*Creating Work Environments Where People Thrive*

S0-BCO-595

# THE BUSINESS
# OF KINDNESS

The Business of Kindness

# THE BUSINESS OF KINDNESS

## Creating Work Environments Where People Thrive

## OLIVIA MCIVOR

FAIRWINDS PRESS

**Copyright © 2006 by Olivia McIvor**

All rights reserved. No part of this publication may be reproduced, distributed or transimitted in any form or by any means including photocopying, recording or other electronic or mechanical methods, without the prior written consent of the publisher, except in the case of brief quotations in critical articles or reviews. For information contact: FairWinds Press P.O. Box 668 Lions Bay, BC., V0N2E0

ISBN 0-9682149-9-1

**Cover design** Leslie Nolin
**Book Design:** Leslie Nolin
**Author Photo:** Jamie Kowal


LIBRARY AND ARCHIVES CANADA CATALOGUING IN PUBLICATION

McIvor, Olivia, 1959-
  The business of kindness : creating work environments where people thrive / Olivia McIvor.


Includes index.
ISBN 0-9682149-9-1


  1. Quality of work life.  2. Kindness.  3. Interpersonal relations.
I. Title.

HD6955.M375 2006          158.2'6          C2006-902226-7

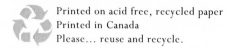
Printed on acid free, recycled paper
Printed in Canada
Please... reuse and recycle.

**Printed by: Universal Printing & Bindery ltd.**

*"This may well be the most important business book published in a very long time. As any good manager will tell you, a company can only succeed as far as its people can take it. Olivia McIvor has put her finger on the crucial yet all to often missing key ingredient to building an enthusiastic, cohesive and productive team. We all are, after all is said in done, not just component parts, colleagues, employees, team members or partners, we are people; individuals who hunger for connection and the joy of collaborative effort.*

*People think that kindness is something soft and squishy and has no place in the rough and tumble world of business. They are exactly wrong. Kindness is extraordinarily powerful, the one sustainable ingredient that can inspire people to bond, engage and excel.*
*The Business of Kindness is the primer that will enable you to create a healthy, satisfying, dynamic, and focused workplace."*

—WILL GLENNON, Author, Attorney, Founder of the
Random Acts of Kindness Foundation, Co-founder of the World
Kindness Movement and current Founder and President of the
Global Classroom Connection

The Business of Kindness

## Dedications

To my brilliant son, Steven
Always give more than you receive,
and know,
there are no boundaries to your potential.

And to my late mother, Alma,
Who days before she passed said to me,
*"In the end, there is only love".*

The Business of Kindness

# The Business of Kindness

CONTENTS

## *Acknowledgments*

Heartfelt thanks to all of the many hundreds and hundreds of individuals in and out of the workplace who have touched my life and continue to make me a better person through their inspiring influence. And special thanks to the following:

Leslie and John Izzo for continuing to lovingly push me past my comfort zones by believing in my capabilities.

Joe Morabito, retired senior vice president, TD Canada Trust, for his visionary thinking and endless support of initiatives that create engaged and safe workplaces.

Story contributors and the past Canada Trust Healthy Living Committee for generously sharing of themselves in the act of kindness for their colleagues and making a difference, one person and one act at a time.

Nadine Marshall, KindActs co-founder, whose patience, love and vision have guided the KindActs movement to stand up and contribute at a national and global level.

Pam Withers for her gifted editing in keeping my voice alive and gently shaping the words on these pages.

Dan Threlfall for supporting me in the initial stages of editing by rounding off my thoughts and words.

The Business of Kindness

# *Preface*

My interest in the "business of kindness" actually began at the other end of the spectrum. I sometimes wonder how I became so interested in a topic like violence in the workplace. Why, of all the areas of focus in my profession, did I find this one the most intriguing? I continued to return in direct and indirect ways to trying to define what "violence" at work really was. I attribute part of this curiosity to the fact that as a human resources professional, I have been granted the privilege to have an inside look at both the positives and the negatives of the workplace. More specifically, because the environments which I have been exposed were predisposed to external violence, I witnessed first and second hand a great deal of trauma in the workplace, which ranged from robberies to domestic violence. Over the years I became fueled by a desire to champion employee health and well-being, with the hope I could make a difference.

At one point in my career, I had worked for one of the world's largest convenience store chains for thirteen years, holding a variety of roles. From managing a store to working in head office positions, I knew there wasn't much I hadn't seen. You meet the most interesting people in the world of 24/7. Some of my experiences will stay with me forever as lessons in human behavior, and some I wish I had never had to be a part of. I was first exposed to the potential for workplace violence while working as a clerk on a graveyard shift. Although I appreciated being trained by the leaders in the industry on robbery prevention, I also felt that additional support was seriously required to train employees in dealing with the aftermath of a serious crime. It was an eye-opening experience to witness humanity in its finest moments as well as in its darkest form.

I have always believed that we have three choices to make when faced with any adversity in our careers, and everyone eventually must face the demon at some point. One is to put a smile on our face, go to work and do the very best we can by making a positive contribution. Secondly, we can choose to quit and go somewhere else. Thirdly, we can put ourselves in a position to influence change. I have tended to take the third option in my career, and as I continued to expand from managing a convenience store to managing human resources departments in various organizations, I always returned to this personal philosophy. I feel a strong sense of purpose and commitment to do whatever it takes to put myself in a position to positively influence change by creating safe and healthy workplaces for my colleagues.

In 1999 I was introduced to a volunteer organization called KindActs that was made up of the most gentle and committed individuals you could ever find. They were driven by a mandate to inspire and facilitate kindness in communities and people's lives. I remember the first evening I was invited to attend a meeting they had arranged to support a couple, Wilma Fuchs and Brock Tully, who had committed to travel ten thousand miles by bicycle across North America to raise awareness for kindness. As I sat and listened to the speeches and enthusiasm, I started to nurture the seeds of an idea to create a "kindness in business" program called Kindness to Colleagues. I took out my pen and scribbled the name on a scrap piece of paper and tucked it away for later consideration.

I spent the next three months trying to figure out how I could possibly introduce this innocuous little word, kindness, into the world of financial banking. At the time, I was employed full time as the human resources director of a large financial institution. To introduce the word was one thing. To not have it dismissed as simply a "warm and fuzzy" concept was quite another. For three months, as I walked back and forth to work, I carefully plotted my plan of how to position the word "kindness" and present it at the boardroom table without getting myself laughed out of the room. Trust me, this could have been an episode; eating live spiders on *Fear Factor* would have been a joke compared to this. I contemplated changing the wording to something less threatening, such as respectful workplaces, caring employer, integrity. You name it, I thought it through, wrote it down, analyzed it and rejected it. All the while I continued to be obsessed with the simplicity and straightforwardness of the word "kindness," because it was universal. Everyone knew what it meant, with little explanation required.

You see, kindness takes words like "caring" and "respect" to the next level —

into action. When we say "be kind" or "show kindness," we understand what that means immediately. We don't require a two-day training program to teach this competency. I realized I needed to find a way to justify this beautiful little word, to find a way to link it to as many of the organizational objectives and initiatives as possible under one actionable roof. I soon realized that kindness was the umbrella that brought all our programs together and, when linked to three themes, it could be actualized: kindness to oneself, to our colleagues and finally to our community. These three themes effectively brought together all of the existing people related programs at the bank. These programs effectively supported and developed all employees, from those on the front line to the executives.

Kindness to Oneself included wellness programs, employee assistant providers, benefits. Kindness to Colleagues brought in existing programs on diversity, sexual harassment and mutual responsibility in the workplace, and expanded them to include the new proactive component of kindness. Finally, Kindness in the Community encompassed all the programs the bank supported and funded in the community, from charity to public relations initiatives.

I realized that I had finally managed to come up with the business rationale for the word "kindness" and now understood how it could be integrated into the existing corporate fiber of an organization. In order to sell the concept to my vice president, I carefully positioned the Kindness to Colleagues concept as a comprehensive retention tool that would effectively communicate, and reinforce to employees, that we offered a great place to work. Once a year, the program would be linked to the company's prestigious regional awards, where the staff's special achievements were honored.

I was fortunate to work for a very progressive regional vice president who gave the concept his stamp of approval. I formed a committee of dedicated individuals interested in championing the kindness initiative, and we immediately commenced the rollout to seventy-two bank branches, ten departments and approximately two thousand employees.

Please don't think for one moment that I am an "expert" on kindness, as I am not sure this is possible for any one human to claim. Nor do I exude warmth and spread kindness, joy and glee to everyone I meet. How I wish this were true, but alas, there couldn't be anything further from the truth. Actually, I can be known as a "to the point" person whose mouth tends to engage before my brain on many occasions. I am not delusional about my own challenges, however. What I believe is that we teach what we most need to learn. Thus was born the concept of the business of kindness and snippets of my own life-long learning that I share in these pages with you, the reader.

# Chapter One
# The History of the Kindness Movement

It's important to set the tone of this book by first explaining how the kindness movement in North America began. John F. Kennedy was quoted as saying, "Every time you stand up for an ideal, you send forth a tiny ripple of hope." Kind acts aren't new to the world, but one woman stood up for an ideal that sent ripples of hope around the world; she was Anne Herbert, a California journalist. Anne Herbert was a columnist during the early eighties who coined a phrase simply by chance that has become one of the most famous quotes of our time. From bumper stickers to key chains, this profound piece of advice reads "Practice random acts of kindness and senseless acts of beauty." Herbert grew tired of hearing news of random acts of violence on the news, something I think we can all relate to. She decided to do something about it and challenged her readers to change this negativity to a positive by promoting the opposite. She encouraged them to go out and commit random acts of kindness.

Her method was simple. Convinced that people needed to hear more good news, she started to write stories about kindness and encouraged her readers to join in by spreading good news rather than negative. Stories of random acts of kindness started to flood in from around North America. Stories told of people paying for the car behind them at a toll both, letting cars in during rush hour, paying for someone's coffee in a café, and on and on.

## Join the kindness revolution

In 1993, Conari Press published a book entitled *Random Acts of Kindness*. I highly recommend it as an inspiring place to start. On the back of the book was inscribed "Join the Kindness Revolution." What at the time seemed like an innocent statement actually led to Conari Press receiving tens of thousands of letters and phone calls from readers saying they wanted to join the Kindness Revolution. In an article, Will Glennon, former owner of Conari Press and executive director of the Random Acts of Kindness Foundation USA, was quoted as saying, "What struck me then and still strikes me now, is that there is a very deep hunger out there on the part of an extraordinarily large group of people to be a part of something that is doing good. In this case it was first and foremost the simple overwhelming need on people's part to feel somehow a part of a compassionate world, to want in some way to be connected." The Kindness Movement has since grown to include over six hundred communities in the USA and Canada alone.

The Kindness Movement also has its roots in other countries around the world. In 1997, the World Kindness Movement was formed at an international kindness conference hosted by the over thirty-year-old Small Kindness Movement in Japan. The founding member countries included Canada, the United States, Australia, Singapore, Japan, South Korea, England and Thailand. The World Kindness Movement was established to acknowledge the fundamental importance of kindness as a basic condition of a satisfying and meaningful life. In order to provide a focus and springboard for the promotion of kindness, November 13 was officially declared World Kindness Day.

Starting a kindness revolution begins with a fundamental, grassroots approach. Here are a number of inspiring individuals who took up the gauntlet, ran with various kindness initiatives and are making a difference in small ways in their communities and workplaces.

Rhonda Taddei from Rhode Island, who integrated kindness into her part of her educational degree assignment, is now a state representative working toward a kindness week campaign and gently slipping kindness into her workplace through in-service training programs. She says, "I am chipping away at it from different angles."

Joanne Morrissey and the Up Your Health Committee from Ontario, Canada, who have been instrumental in the start-up stages of creating a Kindness to Colleagues campaign in their health region by promoting kindness under the umbrella of workplace wellness.

Deborah Dora from Minnesota, who is known as the Ambassador of Kindness in her presentations to corporations, schools and hospitals. Deborah persuades her audiences through her inspiration and enthusiasm to "defy an angry world by becoming ambassadors of kindness in their own lives."

Mari-Lyn Hudson from Alberta, Canada, who created the "heart on the line" kindness award for businesses and community leaders to be recognized for their contributions in creating a kinder world, one kind act at a time.

Susann Castore from Columbus, Ohio, a professional licensed counselor who dons a bright-red floral costume with a cape and mask to match and sets out for local festivals and events. She is officially the A-OK Lady (Acts of Kindness lady) and is known for passing out small yellow smiley face stickers. She believes emphatically "that through smiles we all can connect with one another, if only for a moment."

## The violence continuum

Author Bo Lozoff, leader of an organization called the Human Kindness Foundation, writes, "In the midst of global crises such as pollution, wars and famine, kindness may too easily be dismissed as a soft issue or a luxury to be addressed after more urgent problems are solved. But kindness is in the greatest of need in all those areas, kindness toward the environment, toward other nations, and toward the needs of people suffering. Simple kindness may be the most vital key to the riddle of how human beings can live with each other and care properly for this planet we all share."

This quote has resonated with me since I first read it because of my career in human resources and the "soft skills" dilemma that those in my profession understand as we struggle to promote these skills in the workplace. Soft skills, or people development skills, have not been given the same consideration as the harder operational skills, because of the belief that they don't impact the bottom line as directly as the accounting and loss prevention departments do. We now know that recruitment, retention and training skills are reaching a critical mass. Businesses now believe that these so-called soft skills, these "luxuries to be addressed after the urgent problems are solved," are becoming hard skills trained as a matter of expectation to managers in all businesses.

I have been working subtly and overtly on anti-violence programs in the workplace for years now. By violence, I am referring to the whole continuum, ranging from the way we may speak disrespectfully to one another to the permanence of death. According to an International Labour Organization study, violence in the workplace is on the rise in North America. Perhaps I am naive for believing that if we as co-workers were kinder to and more respectful of each other, many of these acts of violence could be prevented. I am referring to cases of internal violence, where, for instance, an employee uses gossip, racism, or physical, mental or emotional violence against another.

Acts of violence are not committed against organizations, but against real human beings, real people — colleagues and managers who are perceived as not having been supportive. Had these people, already in a vulnerable state, felt more support or compassion from their co-workers or managers, I would like to think these acts of violence would not have happened. In the case of external violence — for example, a bank robbery — a kindness program in the workplace may not directly prevent the specific act of violence. However, such a program would help employees deal with the emotional impact of such acts. I don't think one can fully appreciate how stressful and damaging such events are in an employee's life until one has had the opportunity to see it through the eyes of either the professionals or the colleagues who help these individuals cope with the aftermath of a crime.

Chapter Two

# Understanding the Collapse of Our Workplaces

Recent research indicates that individuals have been faced with continuous change, not only in what they do for work, but also how they work. As information and new technology becomes more available, we increasingly become a "plugged in" society, where people are available at all hours of the day on their cell phones and computers. Our computers have grown from desktops to laptops and now to what I refer to as pocket work, the computer that fits into the palm of one's hand. There is no escape from the world of work.

Because of the rapid and ongoing pace of change, work is increasingly demanding all of the energy and creativity an employee can muster. Management expert Dr. Price Pritchett says that there has been more information produced in the last thirty years than during the previous five thousand. Furthermore, experts estimate that the amount of information available to us is doubling every five years. Is it any wonder that work hours and stress levels are on the increase with this much information to sift through? All this in order to keep from falling behind, while we continue to struggle just to get ahead.

Today's workplaces are faced with the unique challenge of remaining creative and competitive both locally and globally. This is especially challenging in an environment experiencing unprecedented change, while also dealing with the realities of resource shortages, downsizing, multiple roles, increased hours and greater responsibilities.

Author Barbara De Angelis, commenting about our world, says, "In our new global village, we are continually and relentlessly over stimulated, and this sentences us to living in a constant state of subtle, but very real anxiety." I couldn't agree more.

## A trend toward healthy workplaces

One of the most noticeable and alarming effects of the increasing demands in the workplace is the much greater levels of stress, leading to high turnover, absenteeism, increased disability claims, lawsuits and, worst of all, rising incidences of workplace violence. Companies can no longer avoid dealing with what we call the "soft" issues such as stress, training and employee morale. This is because an abundance of research shows that neglecting these issues is significantly debilitating people, productivity and, consequently, profits. No profits, no company. The math is simple, so supporting healthy workplaces is not about draining resources, but rather about sustaining the bottom line.

This realization has led to a positive trend that is picking up momentum and gaining success — the trend toward "healthy workplaces" that share a common vision of linking employee health and well-being to organizational outcomes and the bottom line. While programs aimed at improving wellness are certainly not new, they are picking up momentum across North America. With well-documented success, today's knowledge-intensive workforce requires a more holistic and sophisticated approach to wellness.

David Ulrich, a human resources and business master to many in the ranks of people development, says, "It is the human mind that is the primary creator of value. The quality of people and their engagement will be critical factors in corporate vitality and survival."

To be effective, wellness programs now need to do the following:

* Incorporate coordinated, actionable initiatives that inspire employee buy-in and are woven into the corporate fiber of the organization.
* Focus on bottom-line results by supporting the creation of an engaged workforce.
* Provide a solid foundation with room to grow.

* Establish more positive employee relations.
* Find creative ways to enhance teamwork and creativity.
* Provide a positive effect on employee retention.
* Demonstrate marked improvements in employee surveys.
* Reduce incidences of violence.
* Reduce employee health care costs.
* Increase effectiveness of existing programs through linkages

## The self-inflicted workplace

To discover the impact contemporary changes have had on the workplace and, more importantly, on the worker, I suggest you read a couple of chapters of *The Dilbert Principle*. Cartoonist Scott Adams has truly been able to capture work from an employee's perspective. Although I don't agree with everything he prints, I have to admit that I read his books and subscribe to his online cartoon of the day so I can stay tapped into the perceptions of frontline management.

Through the use of cartoons, Adams has a humorous way of painting management in a negative light, depicting us as self-serving, moronic and incompetent. My question to all of us managers, past and present, is how did we get such a reputation? And even more important to ask ourselves: is it true? Adams says he receives over two hundred emails a day from "disgruntled employees complaining about their managers." He goes on to say, "I will never run out of material as long as there are dysfunctional managers in dysfunctional companies." One day while scanning the Dilbert website, I came across a section where the author explains each of the characters of the comic strip. Pay attention to your reaction as you read the description of the character known only as Boss:

> He's every employee's worst nightmare. He wasn't born mean and unscrupulous; he worked hard at it. And succeeded. As for stupidity, well, some things are inborn.
>
> His top priorities are the bottom line and looking good in front of his subordinates and superiors (not necessarily in that order). Of absolutely no concern to him is the professional or personal well-being of his employees. The Boss is technologically challenged but he stays current on all the latest business trends, even though he rarely understands them.

I have to be honest that I was bit shocked, hurt and disappointed to find these character traits at the foundation of the "Boss." Having been a so-called boss for the majority of my career, I find this portrayal of my peers and myself a bit alarming. At the same time I can attest to hearing similar descriptions of individual "bosses" in my role as a human resources professional over and over again, so I know this perception is alive and well in the workplace. Adams isn't making it up, but basing it on fact. I kept going back, reading this description while reviewing my career as a "boss," wondering if those working alongside me perceived me in this light, for I was sure there were moments when I represented parts of Adams' definition.

I remember being bored on an airplane one night coming back from a long business trip. I was exploring this word "boss" on paper. I have always had a distain for the word and didn't like those working with me to refer to me as their "boss." I preferred to be called a colleague, even though they might report to me on an organization chart. I believe we worked alongside one another. I was interested in really exploring my contempt for this word on paper, and I realized quickly that if you spelled "Boss" backwards, it became "S.O.B." If you left both of the SS's in, it spelled "Super S.O.B" — even worse, don't you think?

The word "sob" brought to mind a reaction I have been forced to counteract hundreds of times in my career, while counseling employees about their managers. Now I know why I dislike the word "boss" so much and suggest that it would be nice to get to the point in organizations where we are never referred to as bosses, but colleagues with different job descriptions and a common goal.

My question to all of us leaders is this — Have we really given Adams such a big stick to beat us up with? How do those who report to me really perceive me? Have they written to Scott Adams to share their experiences? Might that be me in his next cartoon strip? His reach is growing daily; *Dilbert* is now in two thousand syndicated columns and in sixty-five countries.

Thank you, Scott, for providing us bosses with great feedback. I only wish we were able to get it ourselves instead of through a third party.

## Taking responsibility for our leadership role

So much of the condition of our workplaces is self-inflicted by our own management abilities. As I was writing this section it brought back a memory of the day I very clearly suggested to a manager that we were out of ideas concerning his inability to accept the responsibility to change his behavior toward his staff, whom he treated with little regard or respect. Our senior management team had exhausted every technique we knew of. Not knowing what else to do, short of terminating his employment with us, we had run out of conventional options.

As a final resort, I instructed him to do a "non-optional" reading assignment. He was to read the Dilbert book and see if he could recognize himself. He returned at the end of the week and humbly asked me if this is how people perceived him. He was embarrassed and he apologized, saying that he could see his actions depicted in the cartoons. It is one of the most unorthodox methods I have used to get my point across, and I must admit that it came out of a sense of desperation. Surprisingly, he turned the corner almost immediately.

My question to us all is what do we see when we read *Dilbert*? Do you see yourself? Perhaps someone you work for? Perhaps even better, I hope we see someone we consciously never want to become.

## Who's got employee disengagement?

"Employee disengagement is a global epidemic," the headline reads. "New survey has found that only 1 in 7 employees worldwide are fully engaged with their jobs and willing to go the extra mile for their companies." Now that's a bit of a showstopper statistic, isn't it? This 2005 study by Towers Perrin, a global professional services firm with offices in 25 countries and with a client base that includes three-quarters of the world's 500 largest companies and three-quarters of the Fortune 1000 U.S. companies, might have some sound research here to pay close attention to. The study, which is the largest of its kind to date, includes data from 85,000 people working for mid-size to large organizations in sixteen countries.

Donald Lowman, managing director of HR Services for Towers Perrin, states, "What we're hearing is people want to contribute more. But they say their leaders and supervisors unintentionally put obstacles in their paths." The survey defines employee engagement as the measure of an individual's willingness and ability to give discretionary effort in their day-to-day work. We have an expectation as leaders that this level of engagement is being delivered daily, but the research tells us something very different.

One important finding of this study was that more than 8 out of 10 highly engaged employees said they believed they could have a positive impact on the quality of their company's products, whereas only 1 out of 3 of those claiming to be disengaged from their work said the same. On this same note, three-quarters of engaged employees felt they could have a positive effect on the customer service in their organization, as compared to only one-quarter of disengaged employees. Overall the survey indicates that only 14 percent of employees worldwide are engaged in their work. Key elements to creating an engaged workforce include finding ways to instill pride in one's work and helping employees to see the deeper meaning of how their work fits into the bigger picture of the organization's success. Let's not forget also the importance of harnessing the untapped potential of each of the people who work for us.

It behooves us all as managers to take a closer look at the engagement levels in our departments and overall in our organization. The flip side of this is to ask ourselves just how engaged *we* are in our work. How much are we or aren't we contributing within our organization to creating this engaged workforce?

Many people ask me with sincerity if the workplace is this important at the end of the day. I can only emphatically answer yes, because we spend over half of our waking moments in our place of work! We know we must work in order to enjoy the fundamentals of life such as food, shelter, clothing and perhaps even some luxuries along the way. Work also provides us with an avenue to grow our self-worth and confidence through our actions, and provides our primary source of social interaction.

Chapter Three
# We're Walking on Eggshells & Growing Out of Control

During speaking engagements and seminars about the changing landscape of business, I will often compare the people in our organizations to oranges, because I believe it's a great visual. Think for a moment about an orange, with its beautiful gleaming skin, bursting with sweet flavor and juice inside. What happens when you squeeze it? The obvious answer is that you get orange juice. Squeezing brings out the fundamental nature of the orange. In these times of rapid change, when we are squeezing our organizations through downsizing, reengineering, mergers, increased workloads and continuously shifting directions to remain competitive, it is important to ask these question in regards to our people:

* What happens when you squeeze your department, your people, your benefits?
* What do you see coming out? What do you *want* to see coming out?
* And, most important, how can we use these challenges as a tool to create deeper alignment between the organization and the people within it?

To be sure, great things are resulting from this squeeze in areas such as efficiency and effectiveness.

Booker T. Washington knew only too well what squeezing the human spirit could do to dishearten it. But he also was an example of how one can triumph over it. Washington was born into slavery in Virginia in 1856 under intense suppression, yet by 1890 he had founded the Tuskegee Institute in Alabama, becoming one of the most influential African-Americans of his time. One of my favorite quotes of his concerns courage. He said, "If you've already made up your mind to do your best today, you will automatically need courage."

The human spirit, both in the individual sense and as a collective consciousness, has proven its ability to rise to the challenge and meet constant demands. Throughout history there has always been an increased need for flexibility, creativity and perseverance to deliver performance and results. To accomplish this under pressure while being squeezed, one requires a courageous temperament combined with unrivaled passion and purpose. I don't believe that anyone gets up in the morning intending to go to work and do an inadequate or poor job any more than the so-called organization intends to put employees in harm's way. However, perhaps we need to speak more openly and honestly about courage and strength building within our organizations when we are being squeezed by external influences. In my experience, we tend to close our eyes and not discuss the critical issues facing us that would give people the skills to survive these times as a team and triumph.

## Stress: Changing the face of business

It's unfortunate that the annual operations of business that squeeze us on a daily basis are showing themselves in increasing employee stress and potential violence in the workplace. Frank Kenna, president of the Marlin Company, which specializes in workplace communications, publishes his findings every year on a research endeavor called *Attitudes in America*. Concerning workplace stress, Kenna says:

"Half of American workers say that they have a more demanding workload this year than they did a year ago, and thirty-eight percent say they are feeling more pressure at work this year. . . . Stress has become the emotional toothache of the workplace. It leads to serious impairment that can cause big mistakes and serious injuries. As the economy worsens, we need the equivalent of a root canal — employers need to help educate their people on how to fight the infection and ease the pain."

The following statistics are just a sample of the abundance of research that is being undertaken on this topic. These findings come from the American Institute on Stress, the *Occupational Health and Safety News,* and the National Council on Compensation Insurance:

* Stress causes one-third of American workers to seriously consider quitting their jobs.
* 85% of employee accidents are stress related.
* 75% of reported high-frequency illness in employees is stress related.
* Nearly half of American workers suffer from symptoms of burnout, a disabling reaction to stress on the job.
* Some 200 million working days are lost each year because of stress.

In addition:

* A recent Gallup Poll for the Marlin Company indicates that 80% of workers feel stress on the job. Nearly half say they need help in managing stress, while 42% say their co-workers need such help. Yet 65% either say their company has no  program to help them manage their stress or, if it does, they are unaware of it.
* 35% of the Canadian workforce reports feeling highly stressed.
* 43% of Canadian adults aged thirty or over feel overwhelmed by their jobs. Workplace stress causes backaches, migraines and substance abuse — all of which   contribute to poor performance. Chronic stress also leads to hypertension, depression and susceptibility to other common physical illnesses.
* The World Health Organization predicts that by the year 2020, malignant sadness will be the second most debilitating disease in the world.

The following statistics from the American Institute on Stress should be cause enough for any employer to pay attention to proactively addressing stress in the workplace:

* Job stress is estimated to cost U.S. industry $300 billion annually as assessed by absenteeism, diminished productivity, employee turnover and direct medical, legal and insurance fees.

* 60% to 80% of industrial accidents are due to stress.
* Nine out of ten job stress lawsuits are successful, with an average payout more than four times that for regular injury claims.
* 40% of worker turnover is due to job stress according to Desjardins financial securities study
* Stress accounts for $26 billion in medical and disability payments and $95 billion in productivity loss.
* One million US workers are absent on an average workday because of stress-related complaints.
* Stress is responsible for over 40% of the 35 million workdays lost annually because of absenteeism in Canada.
* Statistics Canada calculates the annual cost of work time lost to stress at $12 billion.

## Time to change the shoe

As stress continues unchecked, our people are being squeezed beyond their ability to cope. The result consistently shows up on the bottom line; increased disability claims and absenteeism continue to cause grave concern. Colleagues tell me that stress claims are increasing in all sectors, across all industries. Times are changing, and so organizations must change with them. We need a serious review of our training and professional development strategies to determine whether the programs we were teaching five years ago still apply today.

I have been very privileged to go in and out of multiple organizations across North America each year as a consultant. What continues to surprise me is that the training programs we taught a decade ago remain today, not adapted at all to the changing landscape, their effectiveness seriously diminished. Gloria Steinman, a people advocate extraordinaire, says in regards to learning that "the first problem of us all, men and women, is not to learn, but to unlearn." I am not sure we need "new" programs as much as programs that concentrate on the skills of how to unlearn. If the world of work as we know it is changing monthly, then a revamp of the programs, policies and procedures that support this rapid change must be responsive and change at the same rate of speed. These basic components to enhance one's ability to adapt quickly to change, to promote mental agility and to build resilience by advocating coping mechanisms should be at the pinnacle of our strategic planning.

Steinman has also said, "If the shoe doesn't fit, must we change the shoe?" This is the question I leave us all to contemplate as leaders in organizations going through high levels of constant change. In good conscience, can we merely disregard and discard the very people who built up our organization in its early stages because they appear not to be able to change quickly enough to keep up? Do we let them go too quickly without giving them the necessary skills to adapt, because in our perception the "shoe no long fits"? Do we change the "shoe" or the employee and go get another one that takes less effort? Let's take a step back, review what we have in place to assist them, give them every opportunity to grow, learn and adapt. Then, and only then, when we know there is no other option, should we resolve to change the shoe.

*I have always argued that change becomes stressful*
*and overwhelming only when you've lost*
*any sense of the constancy of your life.*
*You need firm ground to stand on.*
*From there,*
*you can deal with that change.*

—RICHARD NELSON BOLLES

## Chapter Four
# From the Playground to the Boardroom

*Violence in the workplace begins long before fists fly,*
*or lethal weapons extinguish lives.*
*Where resentment and aggression routinely displace*
*cooperation and communication, violence has occurred.*

—INTERNATIONAL LABOUR ORGANIZATION

Every now and then a great quote comes along that makes me really think outside the box. When I first read the following quote by Lindsay Collier, I had to look inward and consider my own opinions and biases and how they have affected my decisions in the past few years. Take a moment and reflect on Collier's quote: "In the past few years if you haven't discarded a major opinion or acquired a new one, check your pulse; you may be dead."

* When is the last time you checked your pulse? Or your department's?
* When is the last time you discarded a major opinion or got a new one?
* Do you think you might be a bit overdue for one?

I use this quote as I begin this section on workplace violence because I am going to make some provocative statements here, statements that for the most part bring two reactions at my workshops and speaking engagements. One reaction is from leaders who insist on informing me there is no violence in their workplace, that the environment is one where everyone is treated equally, with respect and dignity. What I find most interesting is the need they feel to defend their position with me and their tendency to become highly offended at the thought of being challenged. The other reaction happens every time I speak on this topic. I inevitably have a number of people line up to share their experiences of being subjected to violence in their work environment from a colleague or manager, and they always share the grave effects these experiences have had on their health, both emotionally and physically.

What would be your response if I asked you if you thought your workplace exhibited violent behavior? Change doesn't occur overnight, but through one thought at a time. Dr. David Cooperrider, the father of the Appreciative Inquiry model, tells us that the moment we ask the question, change begins to occur. It might not happen overnight, but our minds will not let go of the puzzle and will turn it over and over, seeking a solution.

## Understanding the types of workplace violence

I have witnessed two main categories of workplace violence: external and internal violence. Generally, we don't like to discuss the latter because, as I mentioned above, it's not attractive, nor is it positive and inspiring. On numerous occasions I have been promptly put in my place by both colleagues and executives who claim that there is no violence in their company. I wish I could place my hand on my heart and believe this to be so. If it were, I suppose there would be little point in writing this book, and I would be grateful for this. But the interesting thing is that I have yet to have a frontline employee ever make this statement to me. Curious, isn't it?

One of the most noticeable and alarming effects of the increasing demands and stress of the workplace is this greater propensity toward workplace violence. Almost daily the media reports stories of violence in our homes, schools and workplaces. From personal experience, most of us can attest to the ever-present yet subtle forms of workplace violence, if not to ourselves, then to someone we know. This violence takes on many forms, including bullying and harassment, which over time will erode and slowly undermine one's self-esteem, health and ability to perform effectively on the job.

At least violence is beginning to be officially recognized by a number of businesses and international organizations. Most notably, in 1999, the International Labour Organization, a Geneva-based group, underscored that both physical and emotional violence in the workplace is one of the greatest concerns facing workers in the new millennium.

## Facts on workplace violence

The following facts on workplace violence speak volumes to the effects of ongoing stress resulting from new technology, constant change, increasing demands and lack of job security, just to name a few.

- The International Labour Organization in 1998 estimated that there are one thousand killings in the workplace every year in the United States.

- According to Noah Davenport, author of *Emotional Abuse in the American Workplace*, 4 million U.S. workers are victimized annually by mobbing and bullying at work. Her research also suggests employees waste from 10% to 52% of their time at work defending themselves against bullying.

- The American Institute on Stress reports that there are approximately 2 million reported instances of homicide, aggravated assault, rape or sexual assault in the workplace annually.

Further evidence of the alarming trend toward workplace violence comes from an annual Gallup Poll on American Attitudes in the Workplace, which reports that:

- 14% of workers felt like striking a co-worker in the last year.

- 25% have felt stress to the point of being afraid of losing control by screaming or shouting.

- 10% are concerned about the behavior of an individual in their workplace who they think could become violent.

- 9% are aware of an assault or a violent act in their workplace in the last year.

- 18% are aware of a threat or a verbal intimidation in the last year.

- 12% say they know someone in their workplace who abuses drugs or alcohol on the job.

If those are not enough facts, here are a few more to consider:

- Approximately 2 million assaults and threats of violence occur each year in the workplace (United States Department of Justice).

- In a 1997 British Broadcasting Corporation (BBC) study in the *Leadership Organization Development Journal*, Charlotte Raynor, Ph.D., concluded that 53% of workers reported having experienced bullying and 77% had witnessed it in the workplace.

- Professor Harvey Hornstein, in his book *Brutal Bosses,* estimates that workplace bullying and mobbing happens to 20 million Americans per year.

In a 2006 survey by DesJardins financial security reported 22% of respondents claimed conflict between co-workers & supervisors was the major cause of stress, anxiety and workplace depression.

It's important to take a closer look at the two types of violence, both internal and external; as you read through these definitions, quickly rate your organization and ask yourself whether they exist. Have you ever witnessed any of them yourself?

**External workplace violence** exists in the form of shoplifting, robbery and aggressive or angry customers — in short, any types of violence or acts of force that are being perpetrated by forces or individuals outside the organization. This is the most obvious form of workplace violence and presents the most immediate and pressing need.

**Internal workplace violence** is most commonly manifested as sexual harassment and discrimination based on gender and race. However, the effects of bullying are increasingly being recognized as even more harmful, more widespread and increasingly more costly to organizations.

There are three types of workplace violence, as described below.

**Bullying and harassment** consists of hostile, alienating and unethical behavior amongst employees and employers. This kind of behavior can often lead to more overt violence, as in the case of Pierre LeBrun of Ottawa, Ontario, who opened fire on six of his co-workers, wounding two and killing four before turning the gun on himself. The alleged cause of the outbreak was his co-workers' incessant taunting of his stuttering for years.

**Domestic and personal violence** can spill over into the workplace, threatening the safety of persons not directly involved in the situation. One prominent example involved the estranged husband of a Starbucks employee who entered the coffee shop early one morning intending to kill his wife. The manager, Tony McNaughton, stepped in to protect her and received fatal stab wounds.

**Random or premeditated violence** aimed toward an establishment is usually to retrieve money or goods, but leaves short-term trauma, post-traumatic stress disorder and even death in the wake of the crime. Such is the case when robberies leave fatalities regardless of whether or not anything was done to provoke the thieves.

## The workplace bully

The bullies on the playground have been moving into the workplace since the beginning of time and are exhibiting the same types of behaviors that we saw in them as children. According to Tim Field, author of *Bully in Sight*, bullying can be defined as "the continual and relentless attack on other people's self-confidence and self-esteem." Another author, Gary Namie, who wrote *Bullying at Work*, defines it as "persistent fault finding and belittling." Dr. Heinz Leymann, a German industrial psychologist who has identified and studied the bullying syndrome in Japan, parts of Europe and Australia for over twenty years, refers to it as an "iron fist in a velvet glove," because it is a form of subtle psychological rather than physical violence, one we can cover up as adults. It was only seven years ago when I first started to hear murmurs of bullying in the workplace through articles and the odd comment at conferences I would attend. There was a great sense of relief as I learned more about Dr. Leymann's work and discovered that bullying really did exist, had a name and had been researched for years.

Bullying is perhaps the most prevalent form of workplace violence, not only because it's subtler than the other types, but to a large extent, it's considered to be socially acceptable workplace behavior. I have witnessed repeatedly over the years this subtle form of workplace violence. As managers we were conditioned to "push" people out of the organization by making their lives miserable in the hopes that they would quit voluntarily, so that we wouldn't have to fire them. After all, it was our prime objective to protect company assets, and unfortunately that meant dollars, not employees. I am embarrassed to say that I was trained to use these tactics both as a manager and as a human resources professional for years. All the while, I thought it was good management, until I realized the ethical and moral impact of what I was doing and refused to participate any longer.

I could sense that it didn't feel right, but we can't know what we don't know. Fortunately, education brings with it an awareness that can allow individuals and a workplace to change faster than any other methods I am conscious of. Before I had actually conducted research on this topic and realized there was actually a name for what I was seeing, I had coined it "ganging up on" or "witch hunting" for lack of a definitive word like "bullying." Strange as it may sound, I was relieved to know that what I was seeing was taking place across the globe and had been studied. Now I had a responsibility to speak my truth about it to anyone who would listen.

What I have learned is that bullying leaves employees feeling helpless and defenseless. It leaves many individuals blacklisted in organizations, labeled as difficult or insubordinate, unmotivated, or not a team player. Persistent fault finding and belittling of individuals is common, and victims are forced to tough it out or eventually be "forced" out of their positions through alienation by their managers and their peer groups. They may quit, transfer departments or even cities, be pushed to early retirement through bridging, or end up on short- or long-term disability. In the most serious cases, suicide may even be involved. Dr. Leymann estimated 15 percent of suicides in Sweden are directly attributable to workplace bullying.

North America doesn't gather these statistics, so there is little evidence to support this, but my feeling is that if even one person in all of North America committed suicide because of their workplace, it's one too many, and we should take note. In extreme cases the victim becomes so enraged that they take out their frustration on the employer or fellow employees in lethal ways. Of this we have plenty of examples. Just pick up the paper and start reading. We get angry, blame the perpetrator for committing such atrocities, and yet we rarely pause to consider their side of the story — of how the situation escalated to such a violent degree. Violence is never justified; this is not my point. But we as employers need to take a long look at our practices if this has come upon us. Did we play any part in the emotional and mental collapse of this individual?

## Raising our awareness level

Before we can address the malignant issue of bullying, we must first acknowledge its existence in the workplace, as we did for sexual harassment years ago. I can remember a common explanation when discussing harassment with co-workers or managers. You were told with a chuckle, "Oh, that's just Harry, he doesn't mean anything by it." We accepted it as though it were normal because we didn't know anything else, until the sexual harassment workshops, codes of conduct and educational materials hit from the office towers to the front line. Then and only then were we, the victims of harassment given permission to speak up in defense of ourselves. At the time, we couldn't know what we didn't know. Ignorance is no excuse for unethical conduct when we are all born with a conscience, but I have learned that victims need permission and education to know what is acceptable and not acceptable within the culture of each organization.

Much like harassment, bullying won't begin to decrease until we raise the level of awareness and understanding with both employer and employee. To start the process, research anti-violence and awareness training programs and support their presence in your organization. Take a look at the recommended reading list and program support options included in this handbook. You may find that you can integrate antiviolence programs with existing Occupational Health and Safety initiatives.

Companies across North America have been slow to recognize the importance of taking a proactive approach to help individuals manage stress and anger, resolve conflicts, eliminate bullying and promote strong collegial relationships as an integral part of creating a healthy workplace. Safety is seen as a "hard" issue, whereas stress management is seen as "soft" or not directly related to getting the work done well, on time and without injury. Increasingly this belief is being disproved as research identifies just how closely linked stress and violence are to safety, productivity and profits.

Edward LaFreniere of the Marlin Company links workplace violence to a variety of bottom line issues including health care costs, insurance claims, productivity and retention when he asks: "Why must companies deal with the softer issues? Because they are liable for injuries. Moreover, there's the problem of debilitating morale and productivity, not to mention the potential loss of good workers. No one wants to work in an environment where people are miserable."

Chapter Five
# The Cost of Violence in the Workplace

So how does all this information affect the bottom line? High turnover, absenteeism, disability claims and lawsuits are all outcomes of an organization not paying attention to what is going on right in front of it. Workplace violence and bullying are the results of high degrees of continual stress, poor morale and a lack of zero tolerance policies. In turn, workplace violence and bullying are major contributors to stress in the workplace and can dramatically impact the bottom line of an organization, a double-edged sword.

* According to *CCPA Monitor*, in the United States, 200 million working days are lost each year because of stress, and the cost of treating anxiety-ridden workers tops $3 billion annually.

* The Confederation of British Industry claims that in the United Kingdom, 80 million working days are lost each year to stress, to the tune of £5.3 billion annually.

* Statistics Canada informs us that the annual cost of work time lost to stress amounts to $12 million annually.

These statistics from *CCPA Monitor* are from the year 2000, yet they ring as true today as if they were quoted from 2006. "These trends represent a wake-up call for business," the International Labour Organization says. "For employers, the costs are felt in terms of low productivity, reduced profits, high rates of staff turnover and increased costs of recruiting and training replacement staff."

## Focusing on solutions, not facts

Here are a few tips to consider when working toward a more harmonious and healthy work environment:

**Solution #1:** Create an environment that fosters a sense of accomplishment, celebration and cheerfulness, then acknowledge it every chance you get.

**Solution #2:** Reduce negative behaviors by first identifying what positive and negative attitudes look like in your organizational culture. Hold people accountable to these behaviors by having a low tolerance for toxic behaviors that destroy team spirit.

**Solution #3:** Treat everyone in an inclusive manner by being equally firm, friendly and fair in all your dealings. Teach workplace etiquette as part of your culture expectations.

**Solution #4:** Incorporate an anti-bullying policy into your code of conduct by identifying caustic behaviors, and attach a zero tolerance creed to it with consequences.

**Solution #5:** Foster an appreciative atmosphere, colleague forgiveness and respectful tolerance through open communication.

# Getting on board the wellness trend

As alarming and disheartening as the previously mentioned trends and statistics might be, they are, fortunately, not the only trends and statistics that are changing the face of our workplaces. There is a positive trend picking up momentum — the trend toward "well workplaces" that share a common vision of linking employee health and well-being to organizational outcomes.

Some shining examples of this new trend are recognized annually by the Wellness Councils of America (WELCOA) through their Well Workplace Awards. The Wellness Council started in 1991 and has since awarded over 600 organizations with a stamp of recognition as some of America's Healthiest Companies. For this group, "wellness is no longer centered on random activities, but instead on bottom-line results." These executives are purposefully making resources available to focus on wellness in order to strengthen their people and build their competitive advantage.

In Canada, the National Quality Institute Healthy Workplace recognition program has been giving out healthy workplace awards since 1984. Over 300 Canadian companies have been awarded for outstanding achievement in creating healthy workplaces for employees, with outstanding bottom-line results.

As reported by the Wellness Councils of America, more than 81 percent of America's businesses with fifty or more employees have had some form of health promotion program. As WELCOA states on their website, "More and more businesses are recognizing that, with medical costs potentially consuming as much as half of corporate profits, the bottom line of investing in workplace wellness makes dollars and sense." Furthermore, their research has proven that "cost sharing, cost shifting, managed care plans, risk rating and cash-based rebates or incentives only shift costs." They go on to state that, "Only worksite health promotion stands out as the long-term answer for keeping employees well in the first place."

## Finding positive role models

The following are just a sampling of the accomplishments of healthy workplaces across North America.

**Providence Everett Medical Center** saved an estimated $3 billion (a cost-benefit ratio of 1 to 3.8) over 9 years, with a 28% average reduction in health care utilization during the first 4 years of implementing a wellness program, compared to a control group.

**Du Pont** saw that each dollar invested in workplace health promotion yielded $1.42 over two years in lower absenteeism costs, with absences dropping 14% at 41 industrial sites where the health promotion program was offered.

**The Travelers Corporation** claims a $3.40 return for every dollar invested in health promotion, yielding total corporate savings of $146 million in benefits costs, including a 19% reduction in sick leave over the four-year study.

**Superior Coffee and Foods,** a subsidiary of Sara Lee Corporation, reduced long-term disability costs by 40% with its comprehensive wellness program.

**Steelcase** projects that savings from its wellness program targeting high-risk employees could total as much as $20 million over three years.

On the Canadian front, shining examples are emerging as well:

**M&M Meat Shops'** formal head-office wellness program has achieved excellent results in keeping employee turnover and absenteeism to a minimum while also promoting what they say is the "spirit of professionalism, productivity and teamwork."

**BC Hydro** has been operating a workplace wellness program for over ten years and reports a savings of at least $3 for every dollar spent.

**Canada Life Assurance Company** reviewed the results of its wellness program and found that, over a decade, each dollar the corporation spent on health promotion reaped rewards of close to $7.

**Delta Hotels** has been repeatedly voted one of the 50 Best Companies to Work for in Canada and firmly believes in focusing on health and wellness as an integral part of their culture. They boast of annual improvements in employee satisfaction ratings and increased shareholder profits as a result of this focus.

# Building the business case for a kinder, healthier workplace

If the aforementioned statistics were not enough to drive home the argument for proactive wellness initiatives making good business sense, the Wellness Councils of America outline six important reasons why every business should consider implementing a wellness initiative.

### 1. Health care costs

Americans spend over $1 trillion annually on health care, more than any other nation in the world. Average annual health care costs per person exceed $3,000, but because much of this is linked to health habits, it is possible for employers to affect the bottom line by taking action, via health promotion programs, to reduce health care utilization and their own costs.

Internationally, workplace wellness programs generate a return on investment varying between $1.95 and $3.75 per dollar invested per employee (based on a study conducted by Dr. Ray Shepard for the Canadian government). Integrated disability management practices generate average savings of 16% (1997 Watson Wyatt "Staying at Work" survey).

### 2. Most illnesses can be avoided

Experts suggest that preventable illnesses make up approximately 70% of the entire burden of illness and associated costs in the United States. By leveraging a health promotion initiative, employers can prevent unnecessary illness, ensuring that employees remain healthy and productive while also saving money on health care utilization.

### 3. The work week is expanding

Modern technologies such as modems, laptops, cellular phones, pagers and voice and email have eliminated the boundaries that have traditionally separated work and life, contributing to a steadily growing workweek. According to Harvard economics professor Juliet Schor, the typical American now works 47 hours a week — 164 more hours per year than only 20 years ago. And if this present trend continues, Schor contends that eventually the average person would be on the job 60 hours a week.

Obviously new technologies and the expanding workweek pose a threat to employees in terms of increased stress, higher performance expectations and a variety of other health and well-being issues. A comprehensive and creative health promotion program can help alleviate some of these concerns.

### 5. The technology revolution is on

Since 1983, North American businesses have added some 25 million new computers to the nation's business operations. Our increased reliance on technology has ushered in a whole cadre of new health concerns, including repetitive stress injuries, low back problems and compromised vision. Moreover, because almost one-third of the workforce now spends a majority of their day seated at their desks plugged into workstations, sedentary lifestyles have become a serious health concern that can dramatically affect the bottom line of productivity and health care costs.

### 6. Increasing diversity in the workforce

Increasing diversity in the workforce brings both rewards and challenges. A wider variety of health and wellness issues are involved the more diverse the work group. This demands greater creativity and an ability to be inclusive in addressing these issues.

For these and other reasons, progressive organizations are moving toward teaching stress management skills, implementing flexible work schedules and increasing participation in the company decision-making process. We are learning daily that increasing the quality and quantity of our social interaction in the workplace can also have a significant impact on stress reduction. Regardless of what we decide to do, the programs must be simple enough to be easily grasped and immediately implemented, with a minimum amount of training; otherwise, the stress management process itself will become a source of stress.

# ASKING THE RIGHT QUESTIONS

How does your organization stack up?

_____

_____

_____

_____

Is there room for improvement?

_____

_____

_____

_____

What simple areas could you work on to start creating a safer and more vibrant workplace?

_____

_____

_____

_____

# HEALTHY WORKPLACE SURVEY

If you want to see how your organization stacks up
then take a moment to reflect on these questions.

**Yes?**

1.) Do most departments in your organization experience lower than average turnover, disability claims and absenteeism?

2.) Do stress levels in your organization seem to be decreasing?

3.) Does your organization experience high staff morale at all levels?

4.) Does your organization have proactive, tangible strategies to foster positive working relationships between staff and management, as well as peer to peer?

5.) Do you offer health benefits and actively promote wellness in the workplace?

6.) Do your management and human resources teams have an open door policy?

7.) Are your leaders respected because they have earned it or because of fear?

8.) Is compassion demonstrated by leaders as an example for others to follow?

9.) Is your organization known as a "caring" employer both professionally and personally in the lives of your employees?

10.) Does your organization talk openly and strive to promote life/work balance?

11.) Do you experience consistent excellent communication between management and staff and peer to peer?

12.) Do you have a constructive approach to dealing effectively with negative office politics?

13.) Does your workplace promote a strong sense of respectful community along with "zero tolerance" policies on sexual and racial harassment, safety and honoring diversity?

14.) Do you have an anti-bullying policy and training for both staff and management?

15.) Does your organization have clearly outlined values and vision statements that are fully integrated into every aspect of daily operations at all levels?

16.) Do you help employees explore their talents and assist them to integrate their talents and strengths into their work?

## How does your workplace rate?

* If you answered no to even one of the above questions, there is room for your organization to grow toward a healthier, safer and more vibrant workplace.

* If you answered no to two to five questions, your organization should consider what else it can be doing in this area to become an employer of choice.

* If you answered no to more than five questions, there are probably large opportunities to increase performance and profits in your organization by focusing on enhancing overall employee health, safety and wellness.

## A call to action

Ask yourself what you as a department or organization could STOP, START and SUSTAIN doing to address these questions.

**Stop** doing:

_____

_____

_____

**Start** doing:

_____

_____

_____

**Sustain** doing:

_____

_____

_____

*KINDNESS* in business is simple.

*Always remember before you speak
or take any action,
ask yourself three imperative questions.*

*Is it* **TRUTHFUL**?

*Is it* **NECESSARY**?

*And above all else,*

*Is it* **KIND**?

— OLIVIA MCIVOR

Chapter Six

# Why the Kindness Connection at Work

So how does an organization, or better yet, the individual leader, make the leap from a so-called wellness approach to tabling the word "kindness" at work without being ridiculed out of the room, perceived as someone who is more interested in promoting those things considered "light and fluffy" than the crucial bottom line? Kindness, in my opinion, goes to the heart of the matter.

Our society is built on a foundation of many different types of relationships, which connect individuals to families, friends, work colleagues, communities, countries and our global community. From the playgrounds to the boardroom and into our courtrooms, relationships are at the very heart of our challenges as well as our solutions both personally and professionally. The way we affect each other relates to the quality of our interactions and ultimately determines the health, well-being and success of our employees and our society as a whole.

Leadership is all about relationships, and no matter how hard a leader may try to ignore the fact that their team members are bringing their personal lives to work, the reality is that they cannot be expected to leave a part of who they are in the parking lot. Although this has been the trend for most of our careers, it no longer will fly in the face of the new generations entering the workplace, and the older baby boomers are finally saying enough is enough. Together we will see the workplace take a positive and constructive turn over next few years as the issue of life/work balance comes to the forefront as a recruitment and retention tool.

No matter what our position in an organization, our tenure, job description, pay grade level, gender or our age, it's impossible to expect that we can leave our problems 100 percent behind us when we walk through the door of our office or work setting. In my passion for humanizing the workplace, I am openly defiant about the fact that we have swung the pendulum so far to the left in business that we have discarded our humanity somewhere on the drive to work every day. How is it possible to run a successful department and organization if only a portion of the talent that our people hold is coming to work each day? And is it even fair and realistic to have such an expectation of our fellow colleagues? Is it acceptable to expect us to continue to be human doings instead of human beings?

## Research shows the workforce expects more from us

According to extensive research by Dr. John Izzo and Pam Withers in their leading-edge book *Values Shift: The New Work Ethic and What It Means for Business,* "It's no longer about how workers must adapt to their employers, but how employers must adapt to the new world of work." What is this new world of work exactly and how does it have an impact on the overall heath of an organization? Are these new trends in the workplace supporting the need for improved workplaces with less stress and more of a sense of connection and community?

This groundbreaking study of over two hundred companies across North America reveals six new trends that have an ability to transform the workplace. They are the following expectations:

- ~ Balance and synergy
- ~ Work serving as a noble cause
- ~ Personal growth and development
- ~ Partnership
- ~ Community at work
- ~ Trust

We can see by the words alone the move toward a kinder, more caring workplace is no longer considered unprofessional or "light and fluffy." Trends can be very powerful and can give us the "edge" to recruit and retain the best and the brightest if we choose to listen to their message. I love what the authors say near the close of their book: "Do an honest self-assessment of how you and your company are responding to these shifts, before shrugging off the matter."

## It's okay to hug a colleague

An example comes to mind from the a few years I spent in the world of banking. Where there is cash and an open door for people to walk through, there is a possibility of robberies and violence. During the first year of working there, I realized that there was a serious gap in the training of managers in the area of robberies and violence. We had excellent robbery prevention protocol, and human resources team dedicated to offering support. However, there was little support dealing with the aftermath of a crime, once the employees were left standing with modest support and the leaders not knowing what to say or do next. Concerned, I proceeded to put together a workshop on the effects of robberies on staff, including peer counseling techniques and human resources role in supporting them.

After one particular workshop, a manager came up to me and asked for my opinion on an action she had taken during a particularly harsh robbery. After describing the event to me she said something that to this day echoes in my ears as one of those defining moments. Quietly, she whispered, "Was it okay for me to hug Debra afterwards? She was so upset that I didn't know what else to do. It just felt like what she needed at that moment. I know it's against company policy. Was I wrong?"

*"Was I wrong?"* Those three words hit me with great force, and I assured her that her actions were totally appropriate under the circumstances and she need not apologize for a totally normal reaction in an abnormal circumstance. I made a point of congratulating her for reaching out and demonstrating that she sincerely cared about the pain this woman was in. How odd that her thought was she would be condemned for what she did rather than commended for it. I know this feeling is rampant amongst managers, and she was not alone in her response. Organizations have become so obsessed about creating policies and proce-

dures that we have forgotten the human element in all of it as we aimed to gain control over individual conduct.

As I contemplated my conversation with the manager, I realized that we need to give leaders permission to be human, to reach out to their people in their times of need. We also need to support their better judgment in dealing in whatever way they felt was appropriate to handle the situation at hand. Professional intimacy such as a hug, when done under the right circumstance and with permission from the receiver, was fine. All this takes is good judgment and an intuitive sense of what another human being needs. It is such a shame that we have misplaced our humanity in the workplace somewhere between the desk and our lunch break. I commend Jeff Mooney, former CEO of A&W Restaurants, for saying in a talk to a room full of business executives that as leaders we have to "love our employees if you want them to love our business." Betty Bender puts it this way: "When people go to work, they shouldn't have to leave their hearts at home." I couldn't agree more.

## A hug a day keeps toxicity away

Take Gerry Farrelly of Sutton Coldfield, West Midlands, who is the co-owner of an engineering company that maintains heating devices. After ten years of being in business and with fifty employees, he has fostered a change in their traditional way of doing business by creating a message of "people come first." We've probably all heard this phrase many times before. In fact, it's very trendy now, except in Gerry's case, he has taken it to a new height. Hugs, for example, are encouraged in the office. Socializing and a philosophy of the office never being open past 5:00 p.m. are some other ways he practices a people-come-first attitude.

What is so wonderful about this small company is that hugging is a part of the daily routine. One employee was quoted as saying, "We realize it probably seems a bit strange, but we have found a hug is a superb start to the day and improves communication and bonding." Another employee says this about the 5 o'clock closing time: "It is different here. We are made to feel part of the team, we are pushing in the same direction. Here we all leave together and if someone has work unfinished, we all pitch in to help them get it done so we can all leave." If you are wondering about their financial profitability with the staff leaving so early, you will be pleased to know that since initiating this new caring atmosphere, they have seen profits go up by 200 percent in the past three years.

The impact of efforts to rehumanize the workplace can have a profound effect, yet can't happen without strong and determined leadership. Two particular individuals have had immense impact on me, having forged the belief system and passion for changing the workplace that I have today. I wish I could say that both of them impacted me the same way, but the outcome was the same, and that is what matters. Our teachers are all around us, some insightful, some transparent. Some are examples of what to emulate, while others teach us what to avoid at all cost if we want to have a career with a conscience.

## Wearing my heart on my sleeve

The word "heart" means a great deal to me personally, and as I move about the corporate world using this word freely, I assure you that using this word has not been without struggles and skeptics, being mocked and joked about in meetings. Then again, as public relations professionals will tell you, there is no such thing as bad publicity. We all have turning points in our lives, those moments that define us and in some cases put us on a path toward making a larger contribution. The two individuals I mentioned have had such an impact on me by creating turning points for me, even if they never knew they had. One such turning point in my life came when I had just moved from the Learning and Development department responsible for the training needs of 143 locations. I was now a new human resources manager responsible for the well-being of sixty-five stores, all the while undergoing the usual change and transition of a new role and responsibilities. I was excited and eager to do a good job and make a difference in my market and in an organization that I had grown up in and cared about.

I remember getting my first performance review in my new role and was shocked when I was told that I would never be successful in human resources as long as I continued to "wear my heart on my sleeve." I was told that I needed to toughen up, stop getting so personal with those under my care and not personalize my job. I was then informed that I was too sensitive. Wanting to do a good job, I spent the next year trying to figure out how to stop wearing my heart on my sleeve and to toughen up. I became a victim services counselor, took classes on being a professional counselor, took assertiveness training and worked on keeping a "professional distance," while toughening my stance and body language. All the while I felt like I was betraying my inner voice that told me something was wrong with this picture, that my behavior was causing me to become less engaged in my chosen profession and that this it wasn't what I had signed up for. I was disillusioned.

## Three important pieces of advice from a sage

Fate has an interesting way of bringing us back around when we least expect it, and just as I was starting to seriously contemplate a career change, I attended an annual human resources conference. I was fortunate to sit at lunch with a number of my colleagues, and as we shared stories and experiences, I expressed my dilemma and asked for their tenured advice on how I might solve this mystery of wearing my heart on my sleeve. I was an open book; tell me what to do, please. One of the women at the table, preparing for retirement, asked me to join her outside after we had finished our lunch. As we walked around the grounds of the hotel, she said the words to me that have forged a pathway for my core beliefs as a human resources professional.

She said, in a powerfully assertive voice, "Olivia, everyone will try to make you who you are not, and girl, you will have to fight this battle until the day you leave this world. Trust me, practice every day of your career doing what you do best, wearing your heart on your sleeve. This is a gift, not a curse, and will be the differentiation between you and your colleagues. I have three pieces of advice for you to take away and it's your choice if you choose to accept it, but this is all you need to know to govern your career. If you use them you will be successful." She proceeded: "Before you speak or take action of any type in your work, ask yourself these three questions first. Is it truthful what I am about to do or say, is it necessary that I say it or do it, and lastly, is it above all else kind?" Kindness, she informed me, doesn't mean that you don't have a high expectation of people or don't hold them accountable, but it does mean that every action, be it a hiring or a firing, can be handled with the utmost respect for this person and their self-worth. "Always walk with integrity," she told me emphatically.

We never kept in touch with each other, never exchanged business cards. She simply slipped into my life and out and left a profound message that I strive to carry with me today. Although I have struggled to keep the integrity of her words when I get tossed in the seas of change and pressure, I thank her for reminding me in those dark moments to be myself, for giving me permission to bring my heart to work.

The dictionary describes kindness as "an act or instance of having or manifesting a nature that is gentle, considerate and inclined to benevolent or beneficent actions — suggests gentleness, humaneness and a sympathetic interest in the welfare of others." In hindsight, it now seems strange that I would ever have felt I had to justify using the word "kindness" at work. After reading this meaning, I believe that it should be written as the cornerstone philosophy for all leadership competencies.

## Kindness isn't that complicated

Kindness is a simple concept — too simple, one might be inclined to think, to provide a solution to the complex and serious challenges we face daily in work, not too mention the statistics stated earlier concerning workplace stress and our growing propensity toward overt and covert workplace violence. However, it is precisely this simplicity that allows kindness such power and magnitude to effect change at all levels within individuals and organizations. Promoting kindness in the workplace as a core value only strengthens the foundations of our businesses.

We all know what it means to be kind — how it feels to be the recipient of a kind act — and the rewards of committing a random act of kindness upon another human being. It does not take days of training seminars or piles of manuals to teach people how to be kind to one another. Kindness is something that each and every person knows how to do and can appreciate across all cultures, religions, genders and age barriers.

Although kindness may not be what emerges naturally when people are squeezed by the pressures of work, focusing on kindness as a core value and as a standard for decision-making provides a solid foundation to return to in order to recharge and center oneself in the midst of stress and rapid change. Other, more complex values such as integrity, innovation and creativity are qualities that at a glance are not as easy to grasp. When under pressure to perform and make a choice, it may not be as easy to determine which option represents the highest level of integrity, creativity or innovation, but it is usually quite simple to determine which choice is the most kind to ourselves, our colleagues and our communities.

## Three distinct themes of a kinder workplace

Planting, cultivating and harvesting the seeds of kindness in business is a proactive approach that is aimed at enhancing the health and sustainability of the people within an organization at a grassroots level. We as organizations need to find unique ways to counteract the increasing and often subtle forms of violence in the workplace that create a toxic work environment while simultaneously trying to facilitate the integration of a broad spectrum of organizational initiatives. This next phase of the book is meant to provide methods for supporting a kinder workplace based on these three key themes that support most people initiatives.

*Kindness to Oneself:*
This theme includes self-care, resilience and nurturing of one's inner spirit. By beginning with self-worth and building a strong foundation, one is then capable of expressing kindness to others. The journey begins with self.

*Kindness to Colleagues:*
This theme focuses on treating others with mutual care and respect. It fosters teamwork and looking out for one another through establishing friendships in the workplace. We then can invite others into our circle of positive influence.

*Kindness in the Community:*
This theme looks at making a difference locally and globally through community service. It encourages people to expand their kindness efforts beyond their immediate life and work by giving freely of themselves for others. In giving we receive back.

## The role of the leader is to build character

I used to believe that character was something you either had or didn't, but not something one could cultivate without great struggle. I learned quickly in my career that if this was truly my belief, there was little hope for the humanization of the workplace, and without hope there can be no change; it is what gets us up every morning to do the best job we can. I have taught literally thousands of individuals leadership skills, and when I say "skills," I mean it, because at the end of the day that's all that a trainer can do. No one can motivate you but you. We are each responsible for building our own character and then giving it away. Helen Keller defined character as something "that cannot be developed in ease and quiet. Only through experience of trial and suffering can the soul be strengthened, vision cleared, ambition inspired and success achieved."

Abraham Maslow, the grandfather of the term "self-actualization," has been quoted extensively in business literature because he was so ahead of his time in his understanding that people who were self-actualized lived fuller, happier lives and were more productive. Maslow observed people for a living and determined early on in his career that he no longer wanted to study what was wrong with people, which is the preferred method of the majority of inexperienced managers. Instead, he chose to step outside the norm and study what was right with them. Maslow believed that peak performers had vibrant lives and were fully present in the majority of their actions. He also contended that high-potential performers had what he referred to as "great life indicators." Studying people from varied backgrounds, of varied economic stature and varied health, he discovered that our inner state produced our outer experiences. In other words, we paid attention to what we valued most and inevitably reflected it in our outer world of experiences.

## The wisdom of a great leader

Leadership development is a work in progress. It doesn't happen miraculously when we give someone a promotion and place the crown of leadership on their head and hand them their new business card or the corner office. I believe firmly that every human being has the potential to be a leader and that every single person in this world is a leader to some extent. In everything we say and don't say, in every action we take and don't take, we are leading by example. We hold a responsibility as organizations and leaders to support everyone to talk, walk and act as though they are leaders, to act as though they wear the crown.

I love to tell this story during leadership training programs to illustrate the point that leadership is not a given, but learned slowly as though building a muscle, and we can do so by observing, learning and studying the traits of great leaders before us.

An ancient story is told of a beloved king who was known to his royal followers as a very wise man. He was preparing to turn his kingdom over to his son, the crown prince, but knew that he needed to teach him to be wise first in order to be a great ruler. To do this, the king sent his son into their beautiful forest to live alone for one year. The king instructed the young man that when he returned to the castle, he was to describe the many sounds of the forest to his father.

The boy bid his father farewell and set out into the forest. Over the course of the year he listened for every sound he could hear, and after one year he returned with joy to his father and described the sounds of the forest. He told his father of the leaves as they fell to the ground, of the birds as they sang, of animals of all sizes as they moved through the forest underbrush and in the trees. He told of the waterfalls cascading down the rocks and of the bees buzzing in the air.

The king was not impressed, and with a frown and disappointment he sent his son back to the forest with instructions to listen some more, and only when he was able to discern the true sounds of the forest was he permitted to return home again.

The prince sat alone and despondent in the middle of the forest by a huge tree and pondered his lack of understanding of his father's wishes. Many days, nights and months passed, and the prince became more aware of the world around him. He knew that he could now return to his father with great happiness and honor.

The boy arrived home with much excitement and told his father that he had heard the leaves of the trees as they stretched and awakened in the morning sunshine. He told of the vibrant yellow flowers and how they opened and closed their eyes each day, and how he heard the heartbeats of hundreds of animals and the melodies of the birds singing in harmony together.

The king was very pleased and said to the prince, "My son, to hear the unhearable is the best discipline for being a great leader. The best rulers truly hear the unspoken joys and pains of their people. It is too easy to hear only the obvious and the one-dimensional voices around you, but great kingdoms are built only by hearing the secret sounds of those around you. You have made me proud because you have learned the wisdom of the forest, and your life-long task is to hear the hidden sounds around you."

## Leadership is earned

Leadership is not the right of being born into the role because of tenure or being in the right place at the right time or even less getting a position because of whom one knows. It is not for the person who looks about the room, points the finger when all isn't going well and says "Why don't they fix this problem?" Rather, it's someone who steps up to the plate to fix the problem without being directed. We are each responsible and capable of developing our own leadership skills and talents, thereby making ourselves accountable for managing our own careers. Our organizations are hungry for individuals who are self-directed, personal growth–oriented, with a propensity toward lifelong learning. In my experience, these are the individuals who succeed at all levels, regardless of the position or pay grade they hold. It is true that there is no security in any job — it's in the person who holds the job.

## The twelve character-building traits

As I spoke in organizations and at conferences across the country on the business of kindness, I was repeatedly told, "This is great, Olivia, and I really like the concept, but tell me how to bring the concept of kindness in business to my organization in a tangible way that is understandable and able to make change." As I heard this over and over, I realized that my original thinking lacked the substance to take the concept to the next level. My career in human resources has always been augmented in the learning and development field, an equally strong competency. I set out to conduct my own informal analysis to identify the competency gaps. Where were we failing to train organizations that needed to actualize the value of kindness in our workaday world?

Please know that I haven't done any formal scientific studies, didn't hire a big firm to tabulate, quantify and cross-check my data to ensure it's metrically sound. My assumptions are based on years of experience, training and working with thousands of individuals, on input from colleagues, and on my own personal observations and conversations. I have always found dialogues with real people one-on-one to be equal to if not more robust than statistics.

The Gallup Organization has been doing international research for years on the value of traits and strength development of workers — those areas of our work that are not skills related rather personality related. Gallup puts it beautifully when it says, "Although the approaches of mutual concern, connectedness and respect are profoundly different from traditional wellness interventions, it appears that if they are effectively integrated with these standard approaches, they can have a significant impact on the knowledge of workers' health and productivity."

If we liken ourselves to an iceberg, we choose to see ourselves and those who work with us too simply. Namely, we put too much emphasis on what is obvious above the waterline. These are the parts of the iceberg that we can see with ease, such as the areas on our resume and our skill levels. I call this the "what we are," our credentialed self and the sum total of gathered skills, knowledge and work experience. All the while we forget about exploring and cultivating "who we are," which are our behaviors, values, beliefs and attitudes. How did we forget to hire or cultivate for these innate qualities that drive the skills and resume to success at the end of the workday? The world of work is awakening to this concept of hiring for attitude and traits and training for skills, but we forget that we also have to continue to develop these attitudes and traits once these great people are hired and work with us.

Lifelong learning means exactly that; we have a responsibility to continue to plant, cultivate and harvest the utmost of strengths from everyone under our care. At my local plant nursery a quote that hangs above the entrance reads, "If you're green you grow, if you're ripe you rot." Then there's the classic trainer's quote we have all used for years, "If you want the plant to grow, you have to water it."

There are twelve character-building traits that make up most of the rest of this book. Each trait connects directly to each of the three themes that support creating a kinder workplace. English historian James A. Froude suggests we cannot dream ourselves into a character; but instead we must be willing to hammer and forge ourselves into it. As you move through each of the traits and complete the short exercises, you can't help but build your awareness of each theme and of your own character

*Kindness to Oneself*

Authenticity
Attitude
Resilience
Excellence

| *Kindness to Colleagues* | *Kindness in the Community* |
|---|---|
| Trust<br>Compassion<br>Courage<br>Friendship | Service<br>Responsibility<br>Integrity<br>Tolerance |

*Watch your thoughts; they become words.*
*Watch your words; they become actions.*
*Watch your actions, they become habits.*
*Watch your habits; they become character.*
*Watch your character; it becomes your destiny.*

—FRANK OUTLAW

## The character-building traits challenge

The following sections of this book are meant to be interactive and experiential learning tools that challenge you to think a little differently and build the competency of each of the character traits. The magic of building our character is that we can start anywhere, any-place and to any degree that we want. These traits belong to us at the end of the workday; they are not a commodity that, if given away, disappears. In fact, if you share them, they grow. The following exercises are meant to be interchangeable between our work and home life.

Composer John Cage once described writer's block as "paralysis [that] often comes from not knowing where to begin." When the issues we face in our work and lives seem too overwhelming, let's refer to Cage who suggests that the solution is to "begin any-where." Remember that power is in the present moment in *what* we do; character is *how* we do it and *what we are* at the end of it.

*When was the last time you committed a conscious or random act of kindness*
*to yourself,*
*a colleague*
*or your community,*
*locally or globally?*

*Take the Kindness in Business challenge and commitment a random act of kindness in*
*one of the three themes within forty-eight hours*
*and see how good you feel.*

Chapter Seven
# Kindness to Oneself—Nurturing the Human Spirit

The four character-building traits that support **kindness to oneself** are as follows:

## Authenticity
*honor who you are*

Cultivate awareness of what is most important to you and allow others to see your true self.

## Attitude
*exercise your power to choose*

Develop an ability to look for the positive lessons in your daily challenges by deciding that you are responsible for choosing your attitude.

# Resilience

*develop strong roots to weather change*

Cultivate a proactive approach to creating a healthy and vibrant lifestyle by examining your own behaviors in response to challenging events.

# Excellence:

*commit to grow your potential*

Choose to show up, be present and give 100 percent of your best self to everything you do.

# KINDNESS TO ONESELF SELF-ASSESSMENT

Take a moment to reflect on each of the following questions.
Answer each question with a tick if your response is **yes**.

*Yes?*

Have you patted yourself on the back lately?

Do you consistently ask for you what you need?

Have you stepped outside your comfort zone and rekindled your passion for your work and life?

Have you made contact with a friend or relative you haven't seen in a while?

Have you attended a social event and met new people recently?

Do you nurture your body with healthy foods?

Do you know what you value most in life and do you strive to obtain this?

Do you stretch your mind to new dimensions by reading great books?

Do you take responsibility for your own attitude?

Do you allow people around you to know your true authentic self?

Do you feel like you grow and learn something new every day?

Do you celebrate who you are by treating yourself to something special you want?

Do you always give 100 percent and always strive try to give your best?

Are you proud of the work you leave at the end of your day and proud of your accomplishments?

Do you nurture your body, mind and spirit?

# Authenticity

*Authentic people are genuine and cultivate awareness*
*of their own behaviors,*
*know what they value and live life on purpose.*

*They are not embarrassed to show their humanness toward others.*
*They are consistently genuine and true to themselves,*
*and others feel safe and comfortable in their presence.*

## Authenticity — honor who you are

Years ago I attended a leadership training program on personality styles when one of the key supervisors responsible for a large group of individuals announced with pride that she had no problem "stepping on people to get to the top." I recall sitting there stunned that she was not only in the same personality group as me, but more so that she had been allowed to survive and thrive in the same company that I worked for, not to mention feeling sorry for all those poor individuals she had "stepped" on. I had been openly concerned about all those individuals who reported to her, and I now understood why she had such a high turnover and a less than stellar reputation within her department.

## Are you a right leader or a real leader?

It has been my experience working with leaders over the years that there are really two sides that show and some sides more so than others. We've all met leaders who are externally motivated, somewhat if not predominantly superficial and driven by external influences. By this I mean that they are likely to change their minds based on the last person they talked to and always have a burning need to be *right*. And then there are the leaders, and I mean this in the true sense, who are more authentic, treat others with respect and dignity, demonstrate vulnerability, walk the talk, and therefore people see them as *real.'* This is my language for the two types of leadership within organizations, and it crosses all sectors and positions. If we believe we are all leaders regardless of rank and calling, then this will apply to everyone within an organization.

Margaret Young, an American singer born in the early 1900s, says it best: "Often people attempt to live their lives backwards; they try to have more things, or have more money, in order to do more of what they want, so they will be happier. The way it actually works is in reverse. You must first be who you really are, then do what you need to do, in order to have what you want." I am curious to find out if maybe the *right* leaders have their career objectives a bit in reverse and just don't know it yet. We have probably all heard one of the most quoted quotes in history, Mahatma Gandhi's "Be the change you want to see in the world." I would challenge us all to consider *being the change we want to see in our organizations* first, because if we can't take this philosophy closer to home, then how can we expect to influence the world at large?

Have you ever found yourself driving behind one of those delivery trucks that reads "If this vehicle is not being driven responsibly, please call 1-800 to report"? Today, one out of three people have a cell phone. You can bet the driver takes this quite seriously. I have often wondered what it would be like if as leaders we each had this written at the bottom of all of our correspondence, and those with whom we interface daily could simply pick up a phone and report on how responsible we were, could offer both positive and constructive feedback. It would read something like this. "Hi. I'm Olivia, I would welcome your feedback on my actions and behavior. Please call this 1-800 number and tell me how I am doing."

## Seeking leaders with character

Antanas Mockus is one such leader. He's an example of being the change you want to see. In his case, the change is in his city of Bogotá. His represents one of the most authentic and refreshing leadership stories I have heard in years. Mockus, once a math professor at Colombian National University, decided he needed a new challenge, so he ran for and was elected mayor of Bogotá, a city of 6.5 million people. The city was racked with violence, corruption, street gangs and out-of-control traffic accidents.

You might ask how a guy with no political background gets elected as the mayor of Colombia's capital city. Quite simply, the public felt he was an "honest guy" and they were seeking a leader with character, for a change. Mockus definitely was a leader with character and was known for leading the way through the use of symbols, eccentric humor and life metaphors. The public adored that he was real, while he contended that he wasn't any more moral than anyone else. He spoke freely and openly about his weaknesses; he was vulnerable and it was fine. Mockus was regarded as unusual, and his leadership style allowed him to accomplish extraordinary feats. The streets of Bogotá were extremely unsafe for pedestrians, so he decided to hire 420 mimes — yes, mimes — to control traffic. When he realized how unsafe the streets were for women walking alone, he decided to launch a "Night for Women" and requested that the men stay home one night and care for their children so that 700,000 women could go out with their friends on what was the first of three nights dedicated to women.

And he didn't stop there. He believed that a leader walks the talk, so when there was a water shortage, the mayor went on television and was viewed by millions taking a shower. He demonstrated turning off the water while he soaped down to save water, all the while urging that the citizens of Bogotá join him. The result was a 14 percent reduction in water use within eight weeks. By providing further incentive to reduce water usage, he ultimately lowered usage rates an astounding 40 percent.

If this isn't enough to make us think twice about creative leadership styles, then how about this one? In order to mobilize citizens on an antiviolence campaign, Mockus created what he called the "vaccine against violence" campaign. He mobilized over 50,000 individuals by having them draw faces on balloons of people who had harmed them and then had each person pop their balloons as a symbol of letting go. I can go on and on with more stories from this example of a *real* leader who says emphatically, "I don't like to be called a leader. To me, it is important to develop collective leadership. I don't like to get credit for all that we achieved. Millions of people contributed to the results that we achieved."

I stand in awe of his techniques and results and say to myself that if he can marshal fifty thousand strangers to pop balloons against violence, surely we can inspire our organizations or departments to be a little kinder, to support a healthier workplace. Without question, we can influence the person we are talking to at the moment in the lunchroom. Leadership is about being authentic, being ourselves and above all else, walking the talk. Managers are constantly being judged by the examples they set. We should never underestimate the employee grapevine and its tremendous power.

Lao Tzu, the father of Taoism circa 600, gives us a hint on leadership by saying, "When you are content to be simply yourself and don't complain or compete, everybody will respect you." One sure test of what to look for in a leader is someone who knows the way and starts driving in that direction. If you're not sure about your ability to be a leader and if you want to ensure that you gained the respect of those around you, all you have to do is check the rearview mirror to see if anyone is following you. If they aren't, then you have your answer. Have you checked your rearview mirror lately?

## Wellness programs give people permission to be authentic

It was a strange yet exhilarating feeling to open an email with the agenda attached for the bank branch managers' meetings, only to discover there was a relaxation technique being offered in between the quarterly financial results and a solemn discussion on fiscal responsibility. It was a major breakthrough at the management level to have this on the agenda, let alone at the top of it. Starting a wellness program from a bottom-up approach wasn't easy, and although we had senior management buy into it, it was more from a "don't let it get in the way of your day job" mentality — at least in the early stages, before the results started to bear fruit. Starting a new initiative is somewhat like hiring a new employee — you expect them to prove their worth and value relatively quickly if they want to survive the first few months of scrutiny from their manager and peers.

A dedicated committee of willing hearts and minds committed to making this, our financial institution, an even more astounding place to work than it already was dug in and took the daring route of not only championing a wellness program, but an alternative one at that. We committed to a body, mind and spirit advance, the holistic approach to creating a healthier workplace, and the program was aptly named "the healthy living" program. You could walk into branches and find aromatherapy sprays on desks to alleviate everything from allergies to stress. We held classes from candlelight yoga to relaxation courses as well as the more traditional fitness and nutritional eating and cooking classes that were always popular.

My favorite was the wellness fair, where you could bring your family skating for the day and roam around the booths of thirty-five exhibitors, taste healthy foods, buy personal growth books and even get a massage in between skating sessions. Then there were the workshops for managers that made you just plain laugh at yourself by a local psychologist who was also a stand-up comedian. After all this, to see the fruition of a team's labor of love, where the values were now being integrated into the daily routine of business, made all those long hours worthwhile for everyone. It had started to take hold from head-office and was now spreading to seventy-two individual branches.

To receive an email where a meditation session was being held during a meeting as routinely as the other agenda items was awe-inspiring. Who was it that was going to do the relaxation routine at the managers' meeting? I assumed that an outside individual would be brought in to do this, and so with curiosity in tow, I arrived at the meeting and anxiously sat through quarterly financial branch reporting to see how the managers would take the next item on the agenda. To my utter astonishment, the individual who was going to take us through this meditation wasn't from outside the organization, but one of our very own, a branch manager, one of the group's peers. She proceeded to tell everyone what she was going to do, asked them to close their eyes and for the next twenty minutes, took us all on a stress reduction journey where we placed our worries, our emails and cell phones into a big black box, closed it up and gently pushed it toward the sky.

I truly expected to hear chuckles, see eyes open, hear the rustling of chairs and bodies grappling with the silence and language being used, yet none of my expectations were met. Instead there was calmness in the room, unlimited praise and accolades from her peers for taking them on this twenty-minute sojourn away from the day-to-day stressors of their work. After the day was over, I asked the manager how this quiet time got onto the agenda and where she learned to walk people through mediations so effortlessly.

I soon discovered she had been keeping a little secret from her peers for years. Nancy had been studying to become a hypnotherapy practitioner during her spare time. When I commended her on how courageous she was to express her hidden talent in her work setting, she said that before the healthy living program was introduced, she wouldn't have even considered it. She told me that it was the holistic approach we had taken and the activities that were always going on that gave her the confidence to share a part of herself with her colleagues. The pathway had been opened up for her; it was now safe to do so. This is only one example of what we heard over and over from individuals in all positions within the company, from what I call authentic managers. From the front line to the boardroom, they talked more freely about who they were, not just what they were at work, simply because they had been given permission to bring their whole selves to work again. The gifts to the organization were endless and the magnitude countless.

Do you bring your authentic self to work? Do you have something you would like to share with your colleagues that can improve their day and your own? We all do, and now is the time to find out what the "off work" talents are of those working side by side with us daily. Go ahead, I give you permission, and I promise you won't perish from it, but rather that you will bloom.

## Authenticity is inspiring

The one affirming and consistent message I have been given over the years, after working in all different sizes and sectors of business, is the importance of inspirational leadership. I don't speak just of senior management levels here, as this is only one component of leadership. Great leaders are as important on the front line as they are in the executive offices. In fact, in my experience, they have the majority of the impact in the day-to-day running of the business.

Authentic leadership demonstrates an effortless ability to go well beyond motivating to inspiring those in our sphere of influence. If we take a deeper look into the meaning of these two words — namely "motivate" and "inspire" — we can see that they have distinctly different meanings according to the dictionary.

**Motivate**: *to provide an incentive, move into action, impel*

**Inspire:** *to fill with enlivening emotion; to breathe life into, to draw forth*

Motivating is the first step from which we can begin to inspire people, which can then take the department and the organization to a higher level of engagement and results. Here is my definition of how authentic leaders inspire those around them:

I- *Involve* your people in as much decision-making as you can. Tell them what you know, what you don't know and if you know it and can't say, then be honest and tell them so. People want to be part of a larger vision, so let them join in and support you.

N- *Never* accept less than 100 percent commitment combined with high expectations. Always encourage your people to reach beyond their current level of potential by remembering that accountability plus responsibility equals sustainability.

S- *Stay* the course and hold onto the vision you have created for yourself and your team. Change is constant and can take you off track quickly, co remain vigilant with the vision light so others know where to follow during the dark times

P- *Praise* people every moment you can by catching the positives. Spend your energy encouraging great behaviors rather than wasting precious time looking for negatives. Find ways to rejoice in even the smallest successes by sending the message "You're doing it right."

I- *Insist* upon allowing your values to guide your path. Make it more than obvious to everyone who and what you and your team stand for. Consider it the natural order for each team player to know and be permitted to live their values at work.

R- *Respect* your people by showing them you trust their decisions, judgments and ideas. Allow them to contribute in a fulfilling way by encouraging them to practice their creativity and innovation in a risk-free environment.

E- *Enthusiasm* Sparks lightheartedness. Encourage the spirit of the team through activities that help everyone grow by increasing the positive energy and vitality of the group.

Remember, there is a fine line between inspiration and desperation. Both are consuming, both can lead us down a pathway, and more importantly, both can change lives for good or bad. Is there someone you need to inspire today? Take the time to make a list and create a goal to never go home until you've lifted up another's spirits.

## The road to authenticity starts by defining who you are

Take a moment to reflect on how authentic you are as a leader in your workplace.

**My colleagues at work perceive me to be . . .**

_____

_____

_____

**In my personal life my family and friends perceive me to be . . .**

_____

_____

_____

**At work I allow my colleague to take a glimpse into my personal life and get to know who I am, not just what I do. Please explain:**

_____

_____

_____

**I feel disconnected from who I am at work and who I become when I leave my office because . . .**

_____

_____

_____

**My two greatest contributions to my work have been . . .**

_____

_____

*My top three values in my life are . . .*

_____

_____

_____

*I express my values daily in my workaday world when I . . .*

_____

_____

# MY AUTHENTICITY QUOTIENT

Take a moment to assess your own ability to be authentic in your workplace.
Tick off the statements that are true for you

| check | |
|---|---|
| | I practice honesty, with considerations for others' feelings. |
| | I sincerely respect and encourage the opinions of others. |
| | I avoid putting my ego first at all cost. |
| | I never take credit for something I didn't do. |
| | I am accountable for my actions. |
| | I genuinely care about my colleagues' well-being and happiness. |
| | I work to manage "things" and strive to lead people. |
| | I am trustworthy with my words and actions. |
| | I avoid corporate politics and do what is in the highest and best interest of my colleagues. |
| | I avoid wearing the manager's mask at work and show my real face and expressions when appropriate. |
| | When it's appropriate I show I am vulnerable at work and that I am also human. |
| | There is a big disconnect from who I am at home and who I am at work. |
| | I am willing and able to work with diverse people on my team who supplement areas in which I am challenged. |
| | I have a talent that I haven't shared with my colleagues yet. |
| | I can readily admit when I am wrong and apologize to those involved. |
| | I express myself openly and honestly in all situations. |
| | The people I work with know who I am personally, not just professionally. |

Your assignment, should you wish to take accept it: Bring the list above to your team and have them each fill it out, then allow time for sharing in an open and safe manner.

## A call to action

In order to grow the character-building trait of authenticity, and based on what I have learned about myself, I can support a healthier and kinder workplace if I . . .

**Stop** doing:

_____
_____
_____
_____

**Start** doing:

_____
_____
_____
_____

**Sustain** doing:

_____
_____
_____
_____

*Be original; you have two choices in life.*
*You can dissolve into the mainstream or you can be distinct.*
*To be distinct, you must be different. To be different, you must*
*be what no one else but you can be.*

—ALAN ASHLEY-PITT

# Continuous learning suggestions

Ways to express the character-building trait of authenticity in your life and work include the following:

- ♦ <u>*Write a thank-you note*</u> *to someone who has made a difference to you or someone else at work.*

- ♦ <u>*Take the leap*</u> *and tell your manager you appreciate them and for what reasons.*

- ♦ <u>*Tell colleagues*</u> *what your values are. Hold team meetings and have everyone share what they value most in their lives and work.*

- ♦ <u>*Practice sharing*</u> *more at work of who you are not just what you do. Let others know about your culture, your hobbies, your aspirations and your family.*

- ♦ <u>*Don't say yes*</u> *to people just to please them. Practice saying 'no' to meet your needs by practicing saying what you really feel, and what you want and need to feel engaged in your work.*

- ♦ <u>*Buy a journal*</u> *and write down one hundred goals you would like to achieve in your lifetime. Start making plans to get involved with your life.*

- ♦ <u>*Get outside*</u> *your comfort zone by attending a social event and start by introducing yourself to four new people. Refuse to ask them what they do for a living. Instead, find out who they really are.*

- ♦ <u>*Call a family member*</u> *or friend you haven't seen in a long while and go to visit them.*

- ♦ <u>*Find ways*</u> *to bring your "whole self" to work with all your gifts and talents, and integrate it into your job description.*

# Attitude

*When you see someone with a great attitude, you know it.*
*It's in all they do,*
*from being consistently positive to*
*exuding enthusiasm in their actions and words.*

*People with great attitudes approach life as a classroom,*
*with curiosity and humor.*
*They cultivate a belief that they control their life*
*and that they choose their response to their surroundings.*

## Attitude — exercise your power to choose

## Dancing in the same circle

Most of us don't really think about our vocabulary in any serious way; we just say what we need to say with our existing vocabulary and along the way gather some new words to add to the bundle. Note that the International Listening Organization found that the majority of us have a full vocabulary of 50,000 words. Out of the 50,000, we use approximately 726 words in a typical ten-minute phone call. Research has shown that 90 percent of the thoughts we each had yesterday are the same thoughts we will have today. And since I like to ask questions, I have to ask myself, why is that? Are we so self-limiting without even being aware of it? We're bright people. Why do we keep repeating ourselves? Is it because we like to dance in the same circles because it's comfortable? Are we so enamored with routines that we keep repeating ourselves? Or is it because nobody is listening?

"Nobody is listening" has become a bit of an epidemic in some organizational circles. This isn't surprising when we speak from 125 to 250 words per minute, but we have the ability to think from 1,000 to 3,000 words per minute. It's the gap between thinking and speaking that causes us to lose presence with the person in front of us. Tom Watson Sr., founder of IBM, must have understood this at some level, because in order to continually improve his organization, he had signs posted all over his office that simply read THINK. He didn't want his people dancing in the same circles; he needed innovative and creative people to step outside the box and contribute their talents in a more meaningful way.

## The ability to select our attitude is a choice

We all make a career decision at one time or another in our lives. Mine was to watch people, and to study what was said and how they acted, including my own behaviors in that mix. I have noticed without exception that the individuals who are most successful in work and life are the ones with exceptional attitudes. I wish it were as simple as waking up one day and naturally aligning our attitude to bring us joy and happiness, but this doesn't appear to be the case. In my travels I found that this "attitude" component is an attribute that has to be cultivated, cared for and consistently developed. In many cases it has stemmed from adversity and consciously deciding how one will respond to life's challenges. Do we allow the challenges of life and work to either make us or break us?

Most of us know of Viktor Frankl, famed psychiatrist, who endured unimaginable horrors in Nazi concentration camps. Frankl noted the reaction of the human spirit under horrific circumstances, from both his personal suffering within the walls of the camps and his keen observations of other individuals who were faced with some of the worst possible conditions. Through these observations he was able to bring to the world what is referred to today as Logotherapy, which by definition is "therapy through meaning."

Frankl's book on Logotherapy was appropriately named *Man's Search for Meaning* and was written in 1945 in only nine days. Today it is a classic amongst readers of any genre and has been published in over twenty languages with well over three and half million copies sold. Frankl takes the reader into a concentration camp where every potential goal in life has been reduced to what the Maslow hierarchy of needs refers to as survival instincts, the bottom of the self-actualization pyramid. This is a world where everything in a person's life has been swiftly removed from under their feet, and the little that does remain is what

Frankl calls "the last of human freedoms." He believes it is the last of these freedoms that defined our attitude, our raw ability "to choose one's attitude in a given set of circumstances, the capacity to rise above one's outward fate." His conviction that an individual's life holds potential meaning regardless of the circumstances we are under is the cornerstone of his philosophy. In other words, a firm belief that our "primary motivational force is our search for meaning."

Frankl says that when a person understands the "why's" in their life they can live with and bear almost any "how." We can hardly compare our worst working environment to a concentration camp, but the theory still applies. It gives hope and helps us to understand the importance of communicating the "why's" of our work, these sometimes nebulous circumstances going on around us. People need to know *why* they need to do whatever is being asked of them, and when they get an explanation, they can then explore *how* they can achieve it.

## Victor or victim is a choice

Frankl survived emotionally, as did many others in the camps, because he was able to reframe his life circumstances, make meaning from what seemed meaningless, and shift his state of thought to one as positive as possible under the conditions. It's easy to sign up under the victim banner when life or work throws us a curve ball during a departmental restructuring, mergers, a dysfunctional manager or a colleague that bullies with pleasure, and even when our employment is being terminated. Perhaps we can learn a warm lesson from Frankl on searching for a higher meaning through adversity and choosing to come out a victor.

It is important that we find role models to support our theories of turning adversity into triumph. One such person who comes to mind is Michael Bortolotto, a young man who lives in British Columbia. I had the privilege of meeting Michael when I was volunteering at an event called Clam Chowder for the Soul, a series featuring motivational and inspirational music and speakers. Michael was one of the guest speakers, and I was responsible for ensuring that he got to and from the event on time. As we drove together, Michael referred to himself as a positive rebel, because he had broken the mold of what was to be expected of him. Without question this young man has a gift, not only of being an inspiration, but also of proving to all of us in the auditorium that afternoon that anyone can empower themselves to thrive in adverse circumstances and situations.

As he did his presentation, he mesmerized the audience, made us laugh and cry within the space of thirty minutes by demonstrating that life is about taking positive risks, and he himself had continuously challenged himself to go beyond his personal comfort zone. Michael shared his own unique experiences with us and in so doing taught us a lesson in seeing far beyond our own limitations to our unique abilities. He did this by walking the talk, which is the best teacher of all. You see, Michael has his own limitations; he was born with cerebral palsy, yet he has to date spoken at more than 500 events across North America and to over 45,000 people. A positive rebel indeed. It may be an old trite saying, but attitude really does determine one's attitude in life, so need I say more about making meaning out of life's adversities? Thank you, Michael, for being a powerful example to us all.

## The unintentional language of violence

The "unintentional violence of language" is my term for language that we naturally speak in our everyday lives, language that can appear harsh and actually violent when we really think about it. Think about the following statements and where you have heard these in your workplace and I hope you will understand what I mean. Language such as "bite the bullet," "break a leg," "I would kill for that promotion," "he murdered that report," "I would die for an interview," "don't bring the proposal until you have beaten it to death." How about "If looks could kill I'd be dead," "She annihilated her in the interview," and of course there is "He pulled the trigger on the report I gave him." There's one we have all heard: "We're winning the war." Here are a couple more: "I hate this photocopier," "I'd rather die than do that job," "Execute, execute, execute," and, last but not least, "Meet those deadlines" — yes, DEADlines. Creating a kinder workplace starts in small incremental steps in how we speak. My friend Marcia for years has corrected me every time I say "I would die for that." She gently nudges me in her loving way and says firmly, "No, Olivia, wouldn't you rather live for that?" How right she is, and I am grateful to her for teaching me so much about the power of my language.

I am sure you have thought about the unintentionally violent language of others while you read these phrases, and if so then you get the point I am trying to make. Language is wonderful, it helps us to communicate our collective thoughts and ideas, but it also can be hazardous and risky when trying to convey a message, especially when we are frustrated to the point of anger. It's worth thinking about because when I speak of violence in the workplace, I am not necessarily referring to the end result of someone being driven to physical violence. Violence runs on a continuum and escalates to a serious life-threatening degree only in rare circumstances. In most cases it's the underlying language of hurtful sarcasm, caustic humor and incessant teasing that can transform a department into a toxic environment if there isn't zero tolerance in place, upheld by the leader.

## Workplace etiquette

Perhaps we should think about bringing principles of language etiquette back to the workplace. A college I recently toured had a "code of student conduct" poster at the back of the classroom. The "code" was written on a white board so it could be adapted to each class as they saw fit to enforce it as a group. Each member of the class signed it to acknowledge their commitment to the code. One of the points read, "We will treat each other with respect by supporting each other with positive language." I have been in workplaces where swearing is forbidden and if you curse, you have to put a dollar into a jar to be given to a local charity. Another workplace I know has promoted basic etiquette and returned to pleasantries such as please and thank you, making it part of the job description and performance review. Although many believe this thinking should just be standard operating procedure, and that there is no need to teach people to be polite to one another, I have to challenge this thinking. Watch and listen; basic etiquette is becoming less important in the workplace daily.

Our language is our attitude

Keeping ourselves in check isn't always easy, but is always rewarding. Our commitment to creating a kinder workplace starts with oneself by building our self-esteem through the effective use of internal dialogue first. Individuals who are confident don't feel the need to degrade others with negative language. They create an atmosphere that is both supportive and encouraging.

- What words do you tend to use most often in your workday?
- Do you tend to use the powerful words when faced with a frustrating circumstance or do you revert to powerless words?

Copy this chart and post it somewhere you can look at it each day and tell yourself…

---

...*"Every day in every way I am changing my vocabulary to become more powerful,"*

| POWERLESS WORDS | moving toward | POWERFUL WORDS |
| --- | --- | --- |
| I can't | | I won't because |
| I should have | | I could have |
| It's not my fault | | I'm responsible |
| It's a problem | | It's an opportunity |
| I'm never satisfied | | I want to learn and grow |
| Work is a struggle | | Work is an adventure |
| I hope | | I know |
| If only I | | Next time I will choose to |
| I don't know what to do | | I know I can handle it |
| It's terrible | | It's a learning experience |
| It's not my job | | I'll do it |
| | | |
| **I HAVE TO** | | **I CHOOSE TO** |

## Attitude is a choice

Now that you understand the difference between powerful and powerless words, take a look at your own daily language and set a goal to adjust it. Try practicing for twenty-one days to keep your language in check and see how different and empowered you feel.

Write down four things you **HAVE TO DO** each day at work (e.g., I have to phone the customer back, I have to write the report, I have to do a performance review).

I have to

_____

I have to

_____

I have to

_____

I have to

_____

Now take the same four areas that you wrote above and convert them to powerful language by writing it in terms of **I CHOOSE TO**. Include why you have to do it this time (e.g., I choose to phone the customer back because offering exceptional customer service is imperative to our success).

I choose to

_____

I choose to

_____

I choose to

_____

I choose to

_____

*No thought lives in your heart rent-free.*
*It's either costing you or paying you.*

—ANONYMOUS

## A call to action

In order to grow the character-building trait of attitude, and based on what I have learned about myself, I can support a healthier and kinder workplace if I . . .

**Stop** doing:

_____

_____

_____

_____

**Start** doing:

_____

_____

_____

_____

**Sustain** doing:

_____

_____

_____

_____

# Continuous learning suggestions

Ways to express the character-building trait of attitude in your life and work include the following:

♦ <u>**Create three**</u> *positive affirmations and post them on your desk or workstation, such as: Today I create a great day at work or Every day in every way I am feeling stronger and happier, or I choose this day to be spectacular.*

♦ <u>**Write down**</u> *six things you are grateful for about your work and then get in the habit of sharing them with your colleagues.*

♦ <u>**Practice giving out**</u> *one compliment to a colleague or customer each day.*

♦ <u>**Try to reframe**</u> *any daily negative experiences at work and find the positive gifts in them.*

♦ <u>**Divide a piece of paper**</u> *into two columns and place a plus sign in one column and a minus sign in the other. Write down key influencers in your work and life and whether they have a positive outlook. Ask yourself if you like the company you keep and if you need to change it.*

♦ <u>**Surround yourself**</u> *only with people who are a positive influence in your life. Refuse to invite negative influences into your circle.*

♦ <u>**Write a thank-you note**</u> *to someone who has influenced your life.*

♦ <u>**Refuse to participate**</u> *in victim mentality thinking. Express how you are feeling in a professional manner to the person who you believe has been disrespectful to you.*

♦ <u>**Recommit**</u> *to your personal goals and take charge of your personal life again.*

♦ <u>**Take a creative writing**</u> *course and learn to express yourself through the written word.*

♦ <u>**Leave the chores**</u> *at home and go play with your kids. Leave your work at work and go play with your kids.*

♦ <u>**Take time**</u> *to celebrate who you are and what you have accomplished with your life and in your career.*

*"Assume responsibility for the quality*
*of your own life."*

—Norman Cousins

# Resilience

*Resilient people have strong reserves of inner and outer strength.*
*They are consistently conscious of seeking new ways to build strong personal*
*foundations so they may weather the storms of life and work.*

*Through increasing their awareness of how to care for themselves mentally,*
*emotionally, physically and spiritually, they are able to feel more balanced,*
*accepting change as a natural course of life.*

## Resilience — develop strong roots to weather change

## The human element of change

A few years ago I did a segment for a television series about creating a healthy home environment to support individuals in search of a more tranquil lifestyle, which then transfers to the workplace. We demonstrated techniques for creating a relaxing atmosphere in order to decrease stress levels. One of the production's key aims was to introduce the viewer to various ways they could create a sacred sanctuary within their homes, which might assist them to weather the storms outside within the workaday world. The episode was taped in my apartment to give viewers a sense of how to create a sacred space within a small setting.

This was my first experience with a television production and it was somewhat appealing, as I had never been exposed to this line of work before. I thought since it was meant to run only five or six minutes, the television crew would be in and out in no time and I could get on with my day. My short six minutes of fame took well over three hours of great effort from the three crew, cameras and lights to achieve. Little did I know that what appeared to be an arduously long and painfully slow process was effortless, quick and highly productive in their estimation. I gained a great deal of knowledge regarding the value of perceptions. I learned that what was relaxing for one person can be very stressful for another.

## Daily changes

One of my favorite stories as a little girl was *Alice in Wonderland*, written by Lewis Carroll. In one of Alice's many adventures, she is asked a very poignant question by the Caterpillar.

> *"Who are you?" said the Caterpillar.*
> *"I—I hardly know Sir, just at present," Alice replied rather shyly. "At least I know who I was when I got up this morning, but I think I must have changed several times since then."*

For some us in the workplace, change is an effortless and highly productive time where we are quick to adapt, yet for others it is a long and painfully slow process that seems to take forever. Neither is right or wrong — it is simply a matter of our perception of reality, and it becomes a unique experience for each person.

The majority of us are more conscious of change as one of the major sources of stress in our lives. Change threatens what is most important to us — our control over our environment. The workplace is full of enough changes to set anyone off on any given day. Add in our personal lives and the recipe for a stress cocktail is in the making, except the blend tends to leave a bad taste in our mouth. We tend to go about our daily life within the four-dimensional walls of our organizations, never consciously putting a name to the volume of change continuously going on around us. Here are but a few of the many changes impacting the workplace that I have observed:

- A new department manager
- Reorganizations of responsibilities
- Mergers/acquisitions
- Introduction of new team members
- Project deadlines and hours of work increasing

- Lack of staff or continuous training of new staff
- Introduction of new initiatives
- Changing of culture
- Technology advancements
- New systems and procedures
- Moving office locations
- Strikes and lockouts
- Staff layoffs due to downsizing
- Dramatic changes in policies or procedures
- Job description ambiguity
- New executive changes in organization's direction

These are just a few of the changes in the world of work; I am sure you can think of many more. Although all of these are out of our sphere of influence, we can still learn to control our response to such events by building our resilience to change.

## Perception is reality

Our role as leaders and colleagues during times of change is one of supporting resilience, not pushing against it. Last year I received a phone call from a potential client asking me to speak to a group of leaders regarding mergers and acquisitions. She specifically wanted me to present a list of what leaders should be doing during the transition phase. I suggested I could combine such a list with perspective on the impact, influence and anguish a merger has on individuals. Participants could read the "to-do" list, I ventured, in a book. I told her I preferred to cover such topics as the fallout, the anxiety of not knowing what was coming next, the gossiping, posturing, backbiting, potential bullying, added together with additional workloads and the survivor's guilt common in those left standing after the siege. She agreed these were important aspects of a merger and promised to get back to me, but in the end, her panel decided they wanted me to focus on only the "to-do" list. I declined the speaking engagement because I couldn't in good conscience ignore the critical human issues that a merger raises.

Here are questions we need to ask ourselves to preserve the human spirit during times of change.

- Is there a strong perception within our organization that we care about our people and will go to bat for them?
- What provisions are in place to support our people during a worst-case scenario?
- Do we have a plan for sustaining morale during this time?
- Who can supply this morale-boosting support?
- How can we buffer our people against the winds of the storm?
- Do we have a short-range tactical plan and a long-term strategy?
- What is our method for communicating as we move along?

According to Lewis Mumford, author of over thirty books and considered one of the most original voices of the twentieth century, "Nothing is unthinkable, nothing impossible to the balanced person." The key word here is "balanced." Even when chaos and crisis are occurring around us, there are still avenues we can take to build resistance to stress, such as using all the resources at our disposal to support our team and ourselves. The importance we have as leaders building resistance to change I cannot emphasize enough. It's much like the drill we hear on the airplane before takeoff. "In the event of an emergency, parents should place the oxygen mask over their face first, then assist the child seated next to them." Help yourself first so you can help the people more vulnerable than yourself.

Leaders typically put themselves last when it comes to establishing balance during times of change and transition. If you have experienced work exhaustion, otherwise known as burnout, you know what I mean. It's a very long journey back, and not many leaders return to previous levels of productivity and engagement after burnout. So remember, it's worth securing our own mask first.

Speaking of donning masks to make ourselves more resilient, many years have passed since I came across the following inspirational story. I apologized that I do not know who the author is to credit for this wonderful piece of writing, but I do know it is profound and insightful. This story reminds us of the importance of how our attitude about life events can build our resilience. I hope it has the same impact on you that it had on me.

# A carrot, an egg and a cup of coffee

A young woman named Rachel visited her mother and told her how hard her life was. She confessed that she was so discouraged, she wanted to give up; she was tired of struggling. As soon as she resolved one problem, a new one seemed to arise. Her mother ushered Rachel to the kitchen, filled three pots of water, and placed each on a very hot flame. Soon the pots came to a boil. In the first, she dropped six carrots, in the second she placed two eggs, and into the last, she poured ground coffee beans. She let all three pots sit and boil, without saying a word.

After twenty minutes, she turned off the burners, lifted out the carrots and placed them in a bowl. She spooned out the eggs and placed them in a bowl. Then she ladled up the coffee and placed it in a bowl. Turning to Rachel, she asked, "Tell me, what do you see?"

"Carrots, eggs and coffee," Rachel replied.

Her mother brought her closer and asked her to touch the carrots. She did and noted that they were extremely soft. The mother then asked the daughter to break open an egg . After removing the shell, Rachel observed that the egg had become hard-boiled. Finally, the mother asked the daughter to sip the coffee. The daughter smiled as she tasted its rich aroma.

"What does it mean, Mother? What are you trying to tell me?" Rachel asked. Her mother explained that each of these objects had been boiled in water, and each had reacted differently. The carrots, originally strong and hard, emerged weak.

The egg had been fragile, but as its thin outer shell had protected its liquid interior, it sat in the boiling water until its insides became hardened. The ground coffee beans, on the other hand, had converted the boiling water to coffee.

"Which are you?" she asked her daughter. "When adversity knocks on your door, how do you respond? Are you a carrot, an egg or a coffee bean? The bean actually changes that which would cause it pain as the water gets hot, the bean releases fragrance and flavor. If you are like the bean, then when things are at their worst, you get better and change the situation around you. When the hour is dark and trials are great, elevate yourself to another level."

## So are you a carrot, an egg or a coffee bean?

* Are you the carrot that seems strong, but with pain and adversity, wilts, becomes soft and loses its strength?

* Are you the egg that starts with a malleable heart, but changes with the heat? Did you have a soft spirit, but after a crisis — perhaps a death, breakup or financial hardship — you became hard and stiff? Does your shell look the same on the outside, even though inside you have become bitter and tough?

* Or are you the coffee bean? When things are at their worst, do you get better, make a positive contribution and change the situation around you?

* Is your impact hard or soft?

## Group support builds resilience

Every March in Antarctica as extreme cold moves in, most creatures pack up and migrate north. They leave behind the emperor penguins — the only animal robust enough to spend winter months on open ice. How do the penguins survive? When the temperatures drop, they huddle together in huge circular masses, working as a team to survive. Those on the outer rim of the circle face headlong into minus-100-degree winds as long as they can, then waddle their way deeper into the circle. There they are protected from the icy temperatures as other penguins take their turns on the outer rim. Thanks to this rotational system, they all survive; no one is expected to take care of themselves. Once the resting sentries have warmed up again with the help of group body heat, they put in another shift on the circle's edges.

We could learn a lesson or two from the emperor penguins on the power a team has to support individuals when the winds of change try to freeze our constitution. How much stronger we are when we collectively rally into a circle of friendship to keep each other warm until the weather improves!

# Potential yellow flags of work-related stress

We are extremely vulnerable to workplace stress. Adverse levels occur when we have been exposed for long periods to tense circumstances; we end up constantly on edge. On their own, the symptoms listed below don't amount to much, but when more than three are obvious over a long period of time, this should trigger concern. Protect your colleagues and yourself from mounting stress by heeding these warning signs.

We take a proactive approach to creating a healthy workplace by looking first at our own behaviors. Once we make ourselves resilient and healthy, we can help our colleagues.

| Tick off those statements that apply to yourself and those that apply to members of your team | Self | Teammates |
|---|---|---|
| Do you see yourself or your teammates displaying these signs of distress on a regular basis? | | |
| I have trouble meeting my deadlines | | |
| I generally skip vacations. | | |
| I will skip breaks and lunch due to too much work. | | |
| I feel that my motivation is declining. | | |
| I phone in sick more than usual. | | |
| I tend to leave work earlier than usual. | | |
| I am starting to arrive late for work more often. | | |
| I see a decrease in my effectiveness at work. | | |

*con't*

| | Self | Teammates |
|---|---|---|
| I have been on workers' compensation numerous times. | | |
| I have been on short-term disability. | | |
| I feel I am becoming less reliable at work. | | |
| I have been getting complaints about my performance. | | |
| I feel consistently unreliable to colleagues. | | |
| I am making more errors in judgment than usual. | | |
| My productivity has decreased. | | |
| I have an increasingly negative attitude toward my work. | | |
| I am unusually late for meetings. | | |
| I feel I look strained and tense. | | |
| I am overreacting to minor situations. | | |
| There is a decline in my personal appearance. | | |
| I feel I have to have instructions repeated to me more often. | | |
| I am short-tempered with my colleagues. | | |
| I have decreased lack of respect for authority. | | |
| I am blaming others for errors when they are mine. | | |
| I find myself participating in negative gossip at work. | | |
| I have to cover up my mistakes more often. | | |

# 22 TWENTY-TWO WAYS TO CARE FOR YOURSELF

1. *Exercise on a consistent basis.*

2. *Find simple ways to improve your diet and overall nutrition, such as avoiding sugar, eating a healthy breakfast regularly, and decreasing caffeine and pop intake.*

3. *Find ways to improve your emotional and mental attitude.*

4. *Take more breaks and go for a walk around the block.*

5. *Develop a support network of positive friends.*

6. *Recommit to your personal goals and to yourself; take charge of your life.*

7. *Learn to breathe; practice relaxation techniques or yoga.*

8. *Make a list of realistic to-do's and work at tackling them one at a time.*

9. *Commit to reading articles and books on how to cope with stress.*

10. *Learn to accept that change is a way of life by learning new techniques.*

11. *Try not to spend $5 of energy on a five-cent problem.*

12. *Remember that nothing you do is life-threatening.*

13. *Go for an annual doctor's checkup and get a clean bill of health.*

14. *Explore ways to find meaning in your life.*

15. *Do some volunteer work and help others while helping yourself.*

16. *Commit to spending more time with family and friends.*

17. *Practice methods for venting anger in a healthy, safe and respectful manner rather than holding it in.*

18. *Commit to losing or gaining extra pounds to reach a healthy weight.*

19. *Write down what drains your energy and start to eliminate them one by one.*

20. *Drink at least eight cups of water a day.*

21. *Take that needed vacation or long weekend.*

22. *Follow your talents and interests by taking an evening or weekend course.*

# A call to action

In order to grow the character-building trait of resilience, and based on what I have learned about myself, I can support a healthier and kinder workplace if I . . .

**Stop** doing:

_____
_____
_____
_____

**Start** doing:

_____
_____
_____
_____

**Sustain** doing:

_____
_____
_____
_____

# Continuous learning suggestions

Ways to express the character-building trait of resilience in your life and work include the following:

- *Do one thing* each day that will make you feel alive and in control of your life.

- *Eat lunch away* from your desk — get out from under your workload.

- *Make a realistic* to-do list at work and talk to your manager if your work is getting out of control. Discuss it before you are overwhelmed.

- *Practice* venting your anger in a healthy, respectful way. Speak your truth.

- *Assist a co-worker* who feels overwhelmed and ask them to do the same for you when you need it

- *Take advantage* of your Employee Assistance Program if you have one. Get more detail on it so you have the information when you need it the most.

- *Try once or twice* a week to leave your watch at home and go with the flow

- *Take* the stairs instead of the elevator two to three days a week.

- *Learn to push* back and say no in a professional non-confrontational way.

- *Put the stressful* events in your life into proper perspective. Admit there are very few things in life that are life-threatening, so don't give your energy away to those that aren't.

- *Create a bulletin board* at home and in the lunchroom and fill it with positive items.

- *Practice assertiveness* by asking for what you want and need, in your personal life as well as your professional life.

- *Refrain from magnifying* your small problems by asking friends/colleagues to stop you when you do.

- *Work in nature* and plant a small garden, flower pots or a tree.

- *Treat yourself* to a massage or something comforting and healthy

- *Take a course* or read a book on the power of positive thinking or how to deal effectively with change.

# Excellence

*Excellence is having a firm commitment to grow your potential through being committed to life-long learning. You believe in stretching and challenging yourself by giving 100 percent of your best in everything you do.*

*Take pride in your endeavors both in work and life. Recognize that no accomplishment is insignificant but rather a contribution to the whole.*

## Excellence — commit to grow your potential

## We are our beliefs

Harvard professor Robert Rosenthal is famous for his theory the Pygmalion Phenomenon, which started in the late 1950s as an experiment in an elementary school and continued engaging everyone from college engineering students to air force academy algebra classes. It demonstrates high expectations placed on those in leadership roles and the enormous impact these expectations can have on recipients for achieving outstanding results. The workplace is full of examples from around the globe of research into self-filling prophecies and their effects on individuals, teams and organizational results. One of the most interesting and well-documented studies comes from the early 1900s. It verifies the importance of our beliefs and how they can affect our work environment. This idea isn't new, of course; it has been around for hundreds of years.

In 1890, a tabulating machine much like the electric typewriter was installed at the Census Bureau in the United States. It required very new skills for workers to master the machine. Even the machine's inventor believed it to be quite complicated, so he estimated that trained workers would process approximately 550 cards a day. Initially, the workers did exactly that. As time progressed, they eventually worked up to processing 700 a day, but this caused additional strain. Eventually, management was forced to hire 200 additional individuals to help out on the tabulators. Interestingly, these new workers had no preconceived notion of how many they were to produce or what stress this might induce. So what happened? The new workers started to produce more than 2,100 cards per day without stress, while the original workers continued to produce 700 under great strain.

## Thinking in 100 percents

What makes one person achieve 100 percent while yet another gives only a 60 percent or 80 percent effort? Grab a pen and paper and try out this little equation: Write the alphabet across the top of the page. Directly below each letter place a number. You should have twenty-six letters corresponding with twenty-six numbers. Now spell out HARD WORK, and record how much it adds up to, write KNOWLEDGE and ATTITUDE, and add up the numbers below each. If you add them up correctly, you'll get 98 percent for hard work, 96 percent for knowledge and 100 percent for attitude. Attitude consists of giving 100 percent.

It is this elusive word "attitude" that separates the good from the great. Gustave Leven, the entrepreneur who launched Perrier bottled water in the United States, was told by numerous marketing firms that he was foolish for trying to sell sparkling water in the land of Coca-Cola drinkers. We all know where Perrier stands today, so clearly it's a good thing that Leven didn't take no for an answer and forged ahead.

## Learn your job description, then add to it

Then there's Sparky, an inner-city bus driver with an attitude that would put most of us to shame. Driving a bus isn't easy. A driver's routine involves boredom and the frustration of constant traffic and people flow. But Sparky, as befits his name, has a sparkle in his eyes and an authentic attitude.

I live in the downtown core of Vancouver, where it's much easier to jump on a bus than find parking. I often find myself on Sparky's route. Every time someone boards his bus, he greets them warmly. Anyone exiting gets a shouted goodbye. Once I overheard a customer ask Sparky if he liked his job. "Don't you get bored driving around in a circle, picking up strangers who sometimes aren't always in a good mood?" the passenger asked. Sparky turned with a bewildered look on his face and replied, "I love my job! How could I get bored driving forty of my friends at a time around all day?"

The magic Sparky has is his ability to foster a positive attitude about what he has control over: the total circumference of his bus. He refuses to allow external influences to dictate how he should feel or not feel about his job. Sparky thinks in 100 percents.

Once, while on a business trip in Seattle, I jumped on a bus packed to capacity during a torrential downpour. As the bus started up a hill, the driver grabbed his microphone. I expected to hear the usual cattle-call speech, "Would those standing please move to the back of the bus to make room for more passengers?" Imagine my surprise when instead he said with gusto, "This bus is really full, and I want everyone to turn to the person next to them and make a new friend." For a moment, the skeptic in me thought this demand was going to go nowhere fast, but to my surprise, the entire busload of people did exactly what it was told. We broke into excited chatter. I learned that the elderly lady beside me was a grandmother of three and had lived in West Seattle for twenty-five years. Chatter and joy reigned on that windy, rainy day, memorable for the entire six blocks I rode that bus. I still pause and reflect occasionally on that brave knight, who had the confidence and the 100 percent attitude capable of positively impacting so many lives with one simple command.

Both of these gentlemen exhibited an ability to take positive control of their environments. They choose to make their days valuable by making a difference in the lives of their customers. They accepted their job, learned it well, then took the liberty to add to it.

Nikos Kazantzakis, author of the novel *Zorba the Greek*, strongly advised us, "You have your colours, you have your paint brushes, you paint paradise and in you go." If we take this one step further, we also can paint despair, anger, judgment and apathy. The choice is ours. Choosing to paint paradise, choosing to learn our basic job description — then "writing in" being of service, making people smile, making a difference, going the extra mile — tells me we are far more empowered in the workplace than we realize.

## Building wisely

You meet the most captivating people while traveling, people with whom you might not otherwise cross paths. So while on a flight to Atlanta, Georgia, I struck up a conversation with a man named Paul. I'm not very good at sitting for hours and not getting to know my flight mates. First we exchanged the usual "What do you do for a living?" It turned out he owned a medium-size construction company, and we proceeded to enter into a whirl-wind of conversation. I have come to realize that there are mentors and teachers all around me, and it's my responsibility to seek them out, to learn, and to listen carefully to their stories, for therein lie messages.

After a while, Paul and I started to discuss the importance of giving 100 percent. He kindly shared the following story with me, one that he personally delivers to all his new business recruits. He has been telling this story for the last eight of the twenty years his firm has been in business, which shows he is doing something right. The story goes something like this:

A carpenter getting on in years was ready to retire. He told his employer that it was time to leave construction and take it easy, to live a life filled with leisure and spend more time with his wife and grandchildren. He told his employer that he would miss the monthly paycheck, but that he and his wife would get by just fine. The owner of the company was sorry to see his excellent employee go. He asked if the carpenter would mind doing him one more favor. The firm was very busy at the time, and the owner needed his skills to build just one more house; it was for a young couple. The carpenter reluctantly agreed. Although he built the home, his heart was no longer in his work. He resorted to shoddy workmanship and the use of inferior products and materials. He knew it was a sad way to end a dedicated career, but he didn't really care because it was, after all, his last home. On completion, the carpenter called his boss and told him he could now come over to inspect the house and pick up the keys.

When the owner arrived, he said, "I have no need to inspect the house. This house is my gift to you for your years of dedicated service." He then handed the keys to the carpenter. The carpenter was shocked! The house was now his? What a shame, he thought. If only I had known I was building a house I was going to live in, I would have done it all so differently.

So it is with many of us. Each nail we hammer in, each wall we erect, and each window we install is a house we have to live in. Our work is a do-it-yourself project, and the attitude we choose determines future choices. Peter Drucker, the author and father of business acumen, summed it up poetically when he said the role of a leader includes "lifting a person's vision to higher sights, raising performance to a higher standard, building a personality beyond its normal limitations." So I urge us all to reflect on these questions:

- ◆ What kind of a career are we building that we have to live within?
- ◆ Do we put inferior materials and shoddy workmanship into our day, month or year?
- ◆ Are we going to wake up one day and realize that we have built the career we now have to live with?

As leaders, we are responsible to lift our team and ourselves to a vision of higher sights, a place where giving 100 percent applies, right to the end, in all we do.

## The value of a positive attitude

Do we wonder why we didn't get the raise or promotion we expected, or an outstanding performance review? Much of our work dissatisfaction is self-inflicted, and our attitude can spread to the team. There are four-, six- and eight-cylinder cars; there are also four-, six- and eight-cylinder people. We can't expect the same results from each. At the same time, we should expect nothing less than 100 percent from each cylinder. Anything less is inferior workmanship and fails to support our people in reaching their full potential.

What happens when we expect less than 100 percent? If our expectation is for 99 percent, we'll likely lose that crucial 1 percent. A leader's role is to expect 100 percent, to raise the bar. Joel Barker, author of an innovative book called *Future Edge*, claims that if the workforce lowers its productivity to 99 percent,

- 22,000 checks will be deducted from wrong accounts in the next sixty minutes.
- 1,314 phone calls will be misplaced by telecommunication services every minute.
- 103,260 income tax returns will be processed incorrectly during the year.
- 12 babies will be given to the wrong parents each day.
- 268,500 defective tires will be shipped this year.
- 20,000 incorrect drug prescriptions will be written in the next twelve months.

## Harnessing a positive attitude

A positive attitude delivers excellent results in both our personal and professional lives. Positive and negative attitudes, whatever they might look like to us, are a competency in the workplace. For better or worse, these attitudes control our lives twenty-four hours a day. That makes it imperative that we find ways to keep our attitudes in check, that we keep them balanced so we can achieve positive outcomes. Without great attitudes from the staff working the cash register to those in the boardroom, organizations are like salmon swimming upstream.

Take a moment to think of four people you know with great attitudes. Write down their names and the attributes you feel make them stand out. Having conducted this simple exercise with hundreds of individuals in training programs, I now expect the same main themes to emerge. Here's the universal trait people with great attitudes have in common: They collectively approach people and events with no expectation beyond achieving a positive outcome, plain and simple. This eternally optimistic approach combines innate and cultivated styles. Positive people don't buy into a victim mentality. They don't blame others for their situations; they take responsibility for their own happiness.

So why is it important to hire and harness a great attitude in the workplace? Avoid a toxic atmosphere at all costs. Next, strive for greater engagement, pride in one's work, flexibility and adaptability. Employees with great attitudes tend to be positive mentors and role models to colleagues, and this directly impacts customers' experience as well as decreasing employees' stress and positively benefiting health.

## Finding depth and meaning in work

Robert Fulghum, author of the classic *All I Really Need to Know I Learned in Kindergarten,* says soul is found in the quality of what we are doing. "Nourishing the soul means making sure I attend to those things that give my life richness and depth of meaning," he states.

According to the American Psychology Association, meaningful work is key to healthy companies. With so much talk about wellness in the workplace, it still surprises me that meaningful work rarely makes the agenda past exercise gyms and lunchtime lectures about nutrition. Perhaps we should look at more life-skills training to help employees find deeper meaning and a sense of purpose in their work. It's not a struggle to give 100 percent when we find our work meaningful and in harmony with what impassions us.

## Supporting meaningful work

Everyone needs to feel valued and cherished for the sense of self-worth that encourages us to give our all. It sounds like an easy formula, and quite frankly, in my experience it is. Here are a few suggestions for lifting colleagues up so they can be all they can be.

- Set realistic expectations so the individual can successfully achieve milestones along the journey.
- At all costs, avoid using discouraging, judgmental language.
- Give praise and encouragement generously, consistently and continuously.
- Remember that praise is diminished when you put a "but" in it.
- Demonstrate your respect by hearing what they have to say, and not just when it's convenient.

- Allow each person to be who they are, and accept differences graciously.
- Help them discover their talents and strengths, then build on them. All the while, remember that we all have challenges.
- Allow for creativity, sound decision-making and innovation whenever possible.
- Catch people doing things right at least six times before you utter a critical word.
- Ask their opinion over and over and actually use it, even if only 10 percent of the time.

*Once someone said something nice about me*
*Undeserved though I knew it to be*
*I treasured it there on my heart's deepest shelf,*
*Till one day I quite surprised even myself*
*by honestly making an effort to BE*
*that nice thing that somebody said about me.*

—AUTHOR UNKNOWN

## Jump-starting our attitude

*If someone asked you to describe your own attitude, what would you tell them about yourself? Do you have a positive or negative attitude toward your work and life?*

_____

_____

_____

*Think of various times in which you exhibited positive attitude in your work environment, and relate four examples.*

_____

_____

*Pick a colleague with great attitude and interview them to capture the five attributes that make them stand out.*

1. _____
2. _____
3. _____
4. _____
5. _____

*Write a paragraph about how you felt being around them during the interview.*

_____
_____
_____

Over the course of one month, scan newspapers and magazines searching for as many examples of people with positive attitudes as you can find. Cut out the relevant articles and share them with your team. Create a list of what you believe are the qualities that make up a positive attitude.

# QUALITIES I FOUND THAT MAKE UP A GREAT ATTITUDE INCLUDE:

_____
_____
_____
_____
_____
_____
_____

## A call to action

In order to grow the character-building trait of excellence, and based on what I have learned about myself, I can support a healthier and kinder workplace if I . . .

**Stop** doing:

_____

_____

_____

_____

**Start** doing:

_____

_____

_____

_____

**Sustain** doing:

_____

_____

_____

_____

# Continuous learning suggestions

Ways to express the character-building trait of excellence in your life and work include the following:

- *Explore ideas on how to find a sense of purpose and meaning in your work.*

- *Develop a personal mission statement for your life.*

- *Discover new and innovative approaches to old persistent problems by thinking outside the box.*

- *Start asking yourself where you want your career to be in two years, then five years.*

- *Create a plan for yourself and spend time making it happen. Talk to your manager and ask for their support.*

- *Write down all of your successes from the smallest to largest throughout your entire career since you first started working.*

- *Don't lose sight of what you love about your work. Write down all the positives attributes of your work environment and spend time accenting the positive and letting go of the negatives.*

- *Write down four to five areas of your work and in your life where you are not contributing at 100% and then start a plan to change the percentages.*

- *Find two ways to add to your basic job description and personalize it to your gifts and talents.*

- *Start taking responsibility for your own happiness and being accountable to yourself.*

- *Make up your mind that being happy is more important than being right*

- *Commit to being a positive role model at work and in your personal life.*

Chapter Eight

# Kindness to Colleagues—Creating a Circle of Friends

The four character-building traits that support kindness to colleagues are as follows:

## Trust

*practice honesty with consideration*

Speak your truth with honesty and integrity by demonstrating you are as good as your word.

## Compassion

*show you care with unconditional acceptance*

Practice being nonjudgmental by reaching out to those around you and connecting with empathy.

# Courage
*step through fear to do what is right*

Develop the internal resolve to make a change in your life and do what is right even in the face of personal adversity.

# Friendship
*welcome others into your circle*

Provide a safe and supportive environment full of goodwill and respect for one another.

# KINDNESS TO COLLEAGUES SELF-ASSESSMENT
Take a moment to reflect on each of the following questions.
Answer each question with a tick if your response is yes.

*Yes?*

Do you practice etiquette and good manners at work?

Do you reach out in friendship to a shy colleague?

Do you regularly praise your associates' work?

Do you practice nonjudgment when listening to a colleague?

Do you ever tell your manager how much you appreciate their support of you?

Do you speak your truth consistently?

Do you try to spread positive news and goodwill at work?

Are you committed to not supporting gossip at work?

Do you spontaneously bring a cup of tea to a colleague at their desk or in the lunch room?

Do you greet your colleagues when you come to work in the morning or say goodbye before leaving?

Do you practice being courageous and taking risks for the common good of the team?

Do you share in the not-so-pleasant tasks at work?

Do you honor the differences and uniqueness of each person you work with and treat them with respect?

Do you openly honor diversity in the workplace?

Have you welcomed a new colleague into your group?

**Yes?**

*Learn to listen.*
*You don't learn anything from hearing yourself talk.*

—LEO BUSCAGLIA

# Trust

*You are someone in whom others can confide; they know you will listen without judgment.*

*You are firm, friendly and fair and act with the highest of integrity by always giving credit to those who deserve it. You always strive to be honest, to tell the truth with consideration for the feelings of others.*

*You are known to be reliable and to keep your word*

## Trust — practice honesty with consideration

## Larger-than-life lessons from a shop steward

"You don't want to train with Dean for a week; he'll eat you alive." That was just one of the first comments I heard about the infamous shop steward with whom I was about to embark on a two-year journey. I had decided it was time to cut the umbilical cord and leave a company I had "grown up" in for thirteen years. I was intrigued by the concept of unions and third-party intervention and, being a bit of risk taker, I needed somewhere to test-drive my theories. I was convinced that employees certify with a union when their organizations stop listening, stop paying attention and get complacent — in other words, when trust is dissolved. Yet I also felt that an organization with a union already in place could still enjoy an excellent collaborative relationship with workers — one where the employees' best interests were always first and foremost for both parties. I knew that in order to build trust and enhance collegial relations, I had to first appreciate the union's position. However, I had no idea what this position was.

As I went through the executive search firm interview process, I made it clear I was seeking a company with poor union/management relationships. That, I hoped, would help me explore the truth behind the "us vs. them" mentality so rampant in companies across North America. Trust, I believed, is a lot like a piece of pottery; if you drop it and it breaks, you can glue it back together, even though it will never look quite the same. Trust is one of those words people find difficult to articulate, yet we all seem to know when it doesn't exist in our place of work.

Dean was this piece of pottery: He had experienced a lack of trust between management and employees for years. The pottery was broken; the trust relationships were injured and now seemed beyond repair. He and his union members had just come through a devastating three-month lockout, and the threat of losing an eight-store contract at the airport loomed overhead for everyone if it happened again. I needed to learn the duty-free business as quickly as possible. I had come from one of the world's largest convenience retail store chains, where the average transaction was $250.00. I chose to spend the first few weeks learning everything about the company, from the frontline register to the warehouse distribution centre. It was in the warehouse that I specifically requested to work with the notorious shop steward, Dean. From my very first interview, he'd been described as the guy who would eat me up and spit me out.

I arrived a little nervous for my first shift, early on a Monday morning. Dean and I got our first chance to size one another up. Sizing up is a good description. I'm five-foot-two and Dean is six-foot-two. I have shoulder-length hair, and Dean is bald and tattooed. He resembles a biker. His first warm and welcoming words to me were, "Stay the hell out of my way and we will get along just fine." Then there was the endearing "I don't have any use for you people in human resources." I could see we were getting off to a great start and couldn't imagine what the rest of the day would hold. By the end of our first few days together, Dean had put me through every conceivable part of the operation. I gained an enormous respect for the intricacies of working in a warehouse environment and the attention to detail required for delivering both quality and quantity of service.

Dean, I discovered quickly, was a straight shooter who didn't waste time on words unless there was a need for them. When there was a need, he was usually right on target: precise, to the point, and with sound judgment. This style also worked for me, so within the first three days, I took the liberty of sharing my concerns about his lack of trust and respect for management. It was important to support why he felt this way, but I made it clear that he had no history with me that would indicate I was untrustworthy. I asked a favor of Dean. Would he help me repair the damage that had been done? I assured him that if at any time in our relationship I became someone who in his eyes was untrustworthy, I would step aside and it would be his show to run. In the meantime, I asked, could we agree to be honest and truthful with each other? We shook hands on our deal as two strangers.

Over the next eighteen months, we worked alongside one other, never letting each other down. We had made a promise to each other, and we kept our word. Our collective goals were to repair the irreparable damage; we cleaned up the gray areas of the collective agreement, so the next round of negotiations took only two weeks, a far cry from the previous three-month lockout. We worked on forging closer relationships with the union business managers, better relations between employees and employers, and we educated the managers on local labour laws and the collective agreement, including employer and employee rights. Through many morale-building initiatives and a committed, dedicated human resources team to support the process, we were able to build a respectful and trusting workplace.

I left this organization long ago, but to this day, Dean and I have remained dear friends. It was a friendship forged under the worst of times and the best of times, built on a foundation of possibilities. Dean was a gifted teacher to me, because he was the most authentic person I'd met. I watched his style over those months. He never once stood outside of his integrity on any issue. He called it the way he saw it. He gathered the facts, looked at every situation in an objective and unbiased manner, then spoke his truth with clarity, usually whether you wanted to hear it or not. It was this extraordinary ability of Dean's to be open-minded that allowed me to prove my trustworthiness, which made all the difference. Without Dean we would not have pulled off our outcomes and would not have reaped the outstanding results that occurred. I learned that we find teachers in places where we least expect them.

## Looking for the trust factor

So really, what is trust? I have seen individual managers and entire organizations hunt for the mysterious trust factor. If we think it's something we obtain by virtue of what is on our business card, or by what hierarchical position we hold in a company, we are either delusional or naive. We can't insist that our employees regard us as trustworthy, nor can we stand on our soapbox and decree it from the heights of the corporate pulpit. Trust is something we must shape and cultivate. The sad truth is that when trust dissipates (in an organization or a department), individuals feel they need to look after themselves above the common interests of the group. It pretty much goes downhill from there.

Dr. Duane Tway, in his dissertation *A Construct of Trust*, said, "We all think we know what trust is from our own experience, but we don't know much about how to improve it." The best way to start to rebuild trust in a group is to get the group to define the word "trust"; it's a term that differs by group dynamic or history. There's no cookie cutter definition for trust. To build trust while counseling, ensure that the other person feels her interests are more important than your own. This builds her confidence, a surefire way to achieve trust. Mother Teresa, speaking at an executive meeting, once said in her candid and blunt way, "So you want to change your people. Do you know your people? Do you love them? If you don't know your people there will be no trust, and if there is no trust, there will be no change. And if you don't love your people, there will be no power. If there is no passion and no power, no one will take any risks. And if no one takes any risks, there will be no change."

## Do I have a best friend at work?

The Gallup Organization recently developed an employee opinion survey called The Q12. It technically consists of only twelve key questions, all soundly based on twenty-plus years of research. One of my favorite Q12 questions is, "Do I have a best friend at work?" This question raises lots of skepticism and dialogue among leaders administering Q12, because most of them don't believe that workers' work and personal lives should mingle. Yet ask them what attributes their best friends share and they'll declare, "I don't have to watch my back, they are honest with me even if it hurts, they look out for me, they are there for me when I need them without asking any questions, they care about me unconditionally and — of course, without fail — I can trust them no matter what and they won't lie to me." After working with Q12 surveys for months and teaching hundreds of leaders to do so, I discerned two consistent principles about friendships. They are, namely: trustworthiness and truth telling. In other words, the ability to not lie.

*Do we have a best friend at work?* If so, it doesn't mean we have to hang out with them after hours. But during work hours together, we should endeavor to surround ourselves with dependable people who make us feel safe. The pure satisfaction of knowing that we work next to someone we can both rely on and share our good and bad days with is priceless, both for the individual and the organization as a whole. This sense of security, which comes with trusting relationships, allows individuals and teams to feel comfortable taking risks, and improves upward, downward and lateral communication.

## The value of truth-telling

Where exactly do we draw the line in the corporate sandbox? When is it acceptable to tell a little lie for the sake of what is perceived to be the common good of the organization? We start with innocent falsehoods by embellishing our resumes to get a job. We take a step further to cover a mistake rather than take the heat, and then move on to doing whatever it takes to make a sales pitch or get a promotion. How about the classic "I didn't want to hurt his feelings," to avoid facing the conflict. Or the person who takes a fake sick day rather than saying "I need a mental health day and won't be in today."

Committing to telling the truth is powerful because we don't have to remember what we said or did, and neither do the people who work under our care. As I see it, we have a fiduciary duty as leaders to promote truthfulness within our teams, starting by being a positive example at all costs. Elizabeth Cady Stanton, a leader who played a significant role in the women's rights movement in the United States in the late 1800s, once said, "The moment we begin to fear the opinions of others and hesitate to tell the truth that is in us, are silent when we should speak, the divine floods of light and life no longer flow into our souls."

Where are our souls relative to practicing radical honesty and walking with integrity? As leaders, we have a duty to take stock of our conduct in the sandbox we play in each day. Here are a few questions to consider:

- Do we openly give people permission to tell us the truth without fearing consequences and repercussions?
- Do we have truth-telling expectations embedded into our codes of conduct, values and mission?
- Do we talk openly and honestly with our teams in a safe and inviting environment?
- Do we include training on ethics and truth-telling in our leadership programs?
- Do we clearly draw the line in the sand with a zero tolerance policy that includes consequences for misconduct?
- Do we call our colleagues and ourselves on behaviors that don't demonstrate trustworthiness?
- Do we evaluate the organization as a whole on our ability to be transparent?
- Do we, as leaders, model truth-telling every day in every way?

## What does trust look like to you?

If trust has been fractured like a clay pot, then it needs to be repaired as quickly as possible. However, the journey can take a while, and patience is necessary for everyone. Keep in mind that as a leader, you need to avoid giving people a stick to beat you up with. We need to make every effort to avoid poor communication by making it a habit to tell our people what we know and what we don't know. If we know and can't tell them due to confidentiality, then we need to be honest about this also. Avoid giving misleading information or failing to respond to issues with a sense of urgency. Believe that it is impossible to over communicate.

It is true that as a manager of a department, one can't always control the decisions made by the executive team and boards of directors, but we can take care of our own backyard. We must learn to take responsibility for our contribution, either increasing or decreasing the trust factor on our teams and with our colleagues, because as Gallup says, "Employees don't leave companies; they leave managers."

*What is the turnover like in your department or organization?*

_____

_____

_____

*Write a new description of yourself with the new character-building trait, trust. What would your actions look like in order for people at work to know you are a trustworthy individual?*

_____

_____

_____

_____

_____

_____

*How will you know when you have arrived there?*

_____

_____

_____

# ARE *YOU* A TRUSTWORTHY COLLEAGUE AT WORK?

### Answer these questions using the following scale:

| Strongly disagree | | | | | | | | | Strongly agree |
|---|---|---|---|---|---|---|---|---|---|
| *1* | *2* | *3* | *4* | *5* | *6* | *7* | *8* | *9* | *10* |

My colleagues can expect me to play fair.

My colleagues can confide in me and know that I will listen without judgment.

My colleagues can expect me to be honest and tell the truth with consideration.

My colleagues know that I would never intentionally misrepresent their points of view to others.

My colleagues know they can confide in me and know that I will not gossip about them.

My colleagues know that if I promise to do them a favor, I will carry out that promise.

If I had an appointment with someone, they could count on me to show up and on time.

My colleagues' perception of me is that I am reliable and keep my word.

I always finish doing what I promised I would do, even when I feel like doing something else.

I put my colleagues' best interests over my own.

My colleagues know that I take responsibility for my actions and never blame anyone else.

I treat my colleagues with respect and am fair in all decisions.

I encourage safe and well-thought-out risk-taking and support colleagues if it doesn't work out.

My colleagues witness me practicing integrity and honesty in all my actions.

A call to action

In order to grow the character-building trait of trust, and based on what I have learned about myself, I can support a healthier and kinder workplace if I . . .

**Stop** doing:

_____

_____

_____

_____

**Start** doing:

_____

_____

_____

_____

**Sustain** doing:

_____

_____

_____

_____

*Pretty much all the honest truth telling*
*there is in this world is done by children.*

—OLIVER WENDELL HOLMES

## Continuous learning suggestions

Ways to express the character-building trait of trust in your life and work include the following:

- ♦ *Practice saying please* and thank you consistently while at work.
- ♦ *Commit to only speaking the truth,* in a respectful and kind manner.
- ♦ *Mentor someone* and share your skill, knowledge and abilities with them to help them grow and learn.
- ♦ *Become known* as someone who keeps their word and commitments. Commit to being known as someone who tells the truth.
- ♦ *Give honest* and sincere compliments to your colleagues consistently.
- ♦ *Pass along* a compliment or two to your managers as well.
- ♦ *Refuse* to participate in gossip and conversations that don't support building up the human spirit and self-worth of an individual.
- ♦ *Practice treating* colleagues at work, your friends and family with respect and dignity. Ask them to treat you with the same regard.
- ♦ *Make an effort to* create strong bonds of friendship at work.
- ♦ *Practice listening* without making judgments or forming an opinion.
- ♦ *Practice giving* more than you are receiving in your personal and professional life.

# Compassion

*You are a confident person who offers support without thought of your own needs being met first.*

*Compassion is not about learning to say the perfect things at the perfect time, but rather about showing consideration for others' pain through listening and caring.*

*You see it in a warm, safe smile, a nonjudgmental look of encouragement, a kind touch, or anything that will lift another person to a place of higher confidence.*

## Compassion — show you care with unconditional acceptance

## We are all hurting in some way

I looked up "compassion" in the dictionary when I started to write this section, but not because I didn't know what it meant. Like many people, I know compassion when I see it, but putting it into words is far more difficult. Here is how the dictionary defines it.

**Compassion** *1: a deep awareness of and sympathy for another's suffering  2: the humane quality of understanding the suffering of others and wanting to do something about it.*

I find it interesting that both definitions refer to the word "suffering." So, being curious, I looked up that word next.

**Suffering** *1: troubled by pain or loss  2: very unhappy, fully of misery.*

Not so nice a visual, I thought to myself. Evidently, compassion is such a big concept that the University of British Columbia and University of Michigan started a joint project called the Compassion Lab in 1998. This lab was based on their mutual interest in compassionate acts and their effects on people in the workplace. What they discovered was a striking difference between organizations that demonstrated a high capacity for compassion and those that didn't. In their collective research, they uncovered the fact that this difference has a direct impact on how well an individual recovers from traumatic events in his life, both personally and professionally.

The Compassion Lab's website states that "An organization that doesn't support the healing process risks having its workers question their loyalty." Another report says, "A growing body of research shows when organizations put people first, their performance on almost all indicators is better. In times of trauma, people aren't focused on their job or their organization; they're focused on the pain. But if people are cared for when they're vulnerable, it makes it possible for them to move on more quickly and become more productive again." Yet another report said that "Beyond the obvious, compelling reason of humanity, compassion in an organization lessens suffering, helps people recover more quickly and increases their attachment to their colleagues and the company." In my experience, it doesn't matter so much that a response to one's suffering comes from the top of the organization, although it's better if senior management models this behavior. However, it is crucial that a person's immediate supervisor and the team that surrounds them every day demonstrate compassion. What we say isn't as important as being present for them.

## Saving each other

The September 11, 2001, bombings of the World Trade Center in New York City touched the lives of millions of people. Amongst the hundreds of articles and news broadcasts, one statement stood out for me due to its profoundly simplicity. "We didn't try to save ourselves; we tried to save each other." As both a giver and receiver of compassion in the workplace, I believe that true empathy requires a voice and actions.

## For the love of colleagues

I remember a moment of incredible sadness as I watched thirty multicolored balloons climb into the sky. Rain clouds parted and warm sunshine peeked down. The balloons were filled with handwritten messages from eight-year-olds attempting to put closure on a horrific tragedy that had touched their young lives. Only ten days earlier, I received a phone call to give me a heads-up that one of my managers would be taking time off because her daughter had gone missing. The police suspected foul play. Two days later, her beautiful little girl was found dead in the local forest, murdered violently by a family friend. With all my experience and empathy training, I had no words that could comfort this wonderful, caring and exceptional manager. I could only respond with hugs and tears, joined by all who knew her. All of us wanted nothing more than to support her and her family during this horrific, life-altering event.

I have attended numerous funerals, and sat at the bedsides of dying and ill colleagues. I have filled out more disability claims for stress and critical illness than I care to remember. I have witnessed divorces, addictions, depressions, suicides, workaholics, extremely low self-worth, and every conceivable form of mental and physical illness. In the same breath. I have seen gradual returns to work, births, marriages, graduations, promotions, recovery, life/work balance, health and improved self-confidence. Nothing is static within our organizations. Therefore we cannot afford to be either. It doesn't take much to show that we care, to demonstrate some gentle kindness. As a friend always says to me about our role in life, "We are here to walk each other home." Is there someone in your workplace who needs someone to walk them home?

## With whom would you change your life?

While visiting Stanford University in California a few years ago, I happened to wander into the spectacular and grand memorial church, where carved into the interior sandstone walls was an amazing array of inspirational quotes collected by Lady Jane Stanford. Facing the west wall were these words:

There are but few on earth free from cares, none but carry burdens of sorrow, and if all were asked to make a package of their troubles, and throw this package on a common pile, and then were asked to go and choose a package which they were willing to bear, all would select their own package again. Your heartaches may be great, burdens heavy, but look about you, and with whom would you change?

It's a question I ponder myself: "Look about you, and with whom would you change your life?"

We are the sum total of all of our experiences, both good and bad, but they have made us who we are and who we show up as at our place of work. Life happens while we earn a living, and so to force individuals to suppress their lives at work makes no sense. Sometimes all that is required to allow an individual to unburden his load is to let him talk for twenty minutes. These twenty minutes can save us hours of lost time in the long run. We need to be encouraged to bring our souls to work, to wear our hearts on our sleeves, to be kinder and to teach forgiveness when colleagues have hurt or offended us. And yes, we even need to hug each other in a professional manner when the situation seems to call for that — not just because it's "nice," but because it would serve us all better if compassion were made a core value and competency for the tremendous work we do as leaders.

## Compassion has a far reach

The University of Michigan Business School recently conducted a study called "What Good Is Compassion at Work?" Jane Dutton, the prime researcher on this project and a professor of organizational behavior at the university, has identified what she refers to as a cascading effect — what occurs when a worker experiences compassion in the workplace. Compassion can create a positive effect on the individual and their attitude toward their job, cascading out from there.

Dutton says, "Our findings suggest that compassion among co-workers is more than simply a momentary, humane response to pain; it fosters important organizational outcomes and leaves its imprint on the organizational landscape." What does the landscape of your organization look like? What about the department for which you are responsible?

Dutton analyzed a large community hospital, gathering 171 stories of workplace compassion topped off by another 239 responses from hospital staff. This compelling study concluded that compassion does indeed assist co-workers in finding meaning in their work and lives. Dutton states that "when people experience compassion at work — whether they are on the receiving end, the giving end, or simply observing it — these interpersonal interactions serve as powerful cues about the work context."

In Dutton's study, the researchers listed various ways co-workers could demonstrate compassion in the workplace: giving small gifts, offering emotional support, putting in extra time so their colleague could go home to a sick family member, demonstrating empathetic listening, and allowing a grieving colleague to work through their grief while on the job. The researchers found that positive emotions generated by compassion increase job satisfaction, lower job stress, lower turnover and contribute to feelings of well-being and psychological safety. These linkages permeate an organization, impacting its functioning on many levels. "This paper shows that acts of compassion prompt meaning and generate a feeling that seeps into people's attitudes and behaviors at work," Dutton said. "It demonstrates quite powerfully that compassion does, indeed, count."

## Committing random acts of kindness in the workplace

The year was 1999, and as the human resources director for a large Canadian bank, I was responsible for more than two thousand employees in seventy-two branches and departments. We were undertaking a number of healthy workplace wellness programs as well as working toward incorporating initiatives against workplace violence. We had started a campaign called Kindness to Colleagues, which is where the concept for this book originated. Leading up to the week where staff were to commit random acts of kindness for one another, we held a five-week contest that encouraged everyone in the company to nominate colleagues in one of the three theme areas: kindness to oneself, to colleagues and to the community. We gathered inspiring letters from employees of all levels across the region, honouring one another for various kinds of kindness.

Mark Twain said, "One learns people through the heart, not the eyes or the intellect."

It was through these acts of kindness that as an organization we were able to fully actualize the heart and values of what we truly represented. During the Kindness to Colleagues campaign, we gathered many insightful stories, yet one in particular holds a place in my heart. No matter how many times I read this story, I am unable to get through it without tears in my eyes, because I know it is true and I know the impact the compassionate act had on this lovely woman who wrote it.

> It was the saddest day of my life. It was the happiest day of my life. I was working one day in September 1999 and I had received some very bad news. Of course, I was trying not to let my personal affairs affect my business duties. I worked away as hard and as fast as I could, because I was scheduled to leave a little early that day for an appointment. Being as efficient as I am, and with my outstanding abilities in time management, I was able to clear up all my daily duties with time to spare.
>
> As I prepared to leave, LIFE took its toll on me and I could not hold back the tears. I did not want customers and staff to see me in such a way, so I went to the lunchroom to freshen up . . . and that is where fate led me to dear Jessi. She saw my tears flow a river of sadness. Her heart went out to me, but her lips knew not to ask or utter words of worry. I had to leave, so I thanked her for her support and left.
>
> The next day I came to work and oh, what a surprise! There was nothing but a smile on my face all day long . . . for Jessi had placed a dozen yellow roses on my desk . . . and a card that plainly stated "SMILE: today's another day." And she was right. I am ever so grateful for her being there for me and for caring without needing to know why.

People may forget what we said or did for them, but they never forget we took some time and effort to make them feel better. Compassion takes very little effort and costs even less, because true compassion is established in more than our words; it requires an attitude, an empathic facial expression, a glance or even a touch when appropriate. You will know compassion when you see it because it will always lift a colleague to higher ground, even if for a brief moment in time.

## Compassion takes practice

As a victim services counselor for a number of years, I was in charge of supporting the victims of crime as both their counselor and advocate, to move them as quickly as possible through tragic events that had impacted their lives. I was on call one particular night when at 1:00 a.m. I was awoken by my beeper. The police dispatcher was calling me to the police station to attend to a young woman who had been raped in a parking lot when returning to her car. I arrived at the station somewhat nervous and escorted her to the hospital, where she would undergo treatment and specialized care for rape victims.

In theory, I was trained how to handle such cases. I had read the manuals, taken the course and watched the video on rape kits. Yet when actually faced with the reality of having to reassure this young women, I suddenly felt woefully inadequate. My first instinct was to assist her down the steps of the police station and into my car. What I learned that night was to never assume what might be best for someone. As it turned out, physically assisting her was the worst thing I could have done, for two reasons. One, her entire body was in pain from fighting off her attacker, and secondly, the thought of anyone — male or female — touching her sent her back into a fight-or-flight stance to protect herself.

People in pain have been some of my greatest instructors in the human condition, because it's not possible for any one human being to experience all the full range of trials and tribulations around us. It is our duty, however, to be awake, to walk in someone else's shoes, and through their stories to learn how to become more sensitive to others. As a human resources professional, I knew that here was a woman who would return to her workplace in a week, where only a few select individuals, if any, would ever know what had happened to her on that rainy October night in a parking lot. All they would know is that their colleague was away from work for a week, perhaps due to the flu or a family tragedy. They might sense she wasn't herself, but wouldn't know why; even her manager would probably never know why her productivity declined and she seemed so unengaged. They would not be able to fix it or soothe her pain. But they could still be there for her without judgment, without knowing why, and perhaps someone would commit a random act of kindness, like placing yellow roses on her desk.

## Practicing the art of compassion

It takes time to cultivate compassion. We need to be patient and give ourselves permission to reach out rather than shut down when we face something uncomfortable. Any attempt at showing you care is appreciated by those in pain. As one colleague said to me after the death of her husband, "I didn't care if people said anything; I just wanted to look around the chapel and see faces I knew cared about me and my family." In his newest book, *A Spirituality Named Compassion*, author Mathew Fox defines compassion with such clarity: "The difference between persons and groups of persons is not that some are victims and some are not; we are all victims and all dying from lack of compassion; we are all surrendering our humanity together."

When reaching out with compassion to those around us, we need to remember we have a mission to:

- walk beside our colleagues, not to carry them
- listen without feeling the need to speak or fill in words
- assist our colleagues in making choices that are simple to start with
- provide support for their injured spirit, not to take responsibility for what has happened to them
- help them discover their own strength, not attempt a rescue that leaves them feeling even more vulnerable
- help them explore what they are feeling inside so they need not hide their emotions

## The five-penny challenge

I have used this straightforward exercise during training programs, each time with surprising and varied results, from a deep emotional impact on participants to tears or smiles.

**The challenge:** Put five pennies in your pocket, on your desk or somewhere close to you where you can see or touch them easily. Starting off slowly at first, say one penny per week, graduate to one a day and eventually to five a day.

**The idea:** Every time you practice being compassionate — passing along a compliment, positively reinforcing a colleague who did something right, or simply saying thank you — then move a penny into your other pocket or to the other side of your desk. The idea is to keep score with yourself as a reminder to contribute to a more compassionate workplace.

| *Name of recipient of penny challenge* | *How I felt afterwards* |
|---|---|
| * _____ | * _____ |
| * _____ | * _____ |
| * _____ | * _____ |
| * _____ | * _____ |
| * _____ | * _____ |

*If someone were to pay you ten cents*
*for every kind word you ever spoke and*
*collect five cents for every unkind word,*
*would you be richer or poorer?*

—NONPAREIL

# A call to action

In order to grow the character-building trait of compassion, and based on what I have learned about myself, I can support a healthier and kinder workplace if I . . .

**Stop** doing:

_____

_____

_____

_____

**Start** doing:

_____

_____

_____

_____

**Sustain** doing:

_____

_____

_____

_____

*Be compassionate. It is the sure way to*
*understanding and acceptance.*

—LEO BUSCAGLIA

# Continuous learning suggestions

Ways to express the character-building trait of compassion in your life and work include the following:

- *Actively listen* to a colleague when they are seeking your input and remain non-judgmental and accepting of their thoughts and ideas.

- *Be sensitive* to colleagues' successes as well as their challenges.

- *If a colleague seems* overwhelmed with their workload, talk to them and offer suggestions or offer to assist them.

- *Remember* what it was like to be a new employee and welcome new recruits into your circle of friends at work.

- *Get involved* in your community to learn compassion for others.

- *If a colleague* is in emotional pain ask them if they need a hug and give it.

- *Find ways* to compliment and praise others' efforts consistently.

- *Become available* and mean it even if it's not always convenient for you.

- *Place people* before tasks by giving them an acceptable amount of your time when they request it.

- *Stop what you are doing* by demonstrating active listening skills, eye contact and body language that show you are present.

- *Don't avoid uncomfortable* situations just because you don't know what to say. Actions speak louder than words.

- *Spend quality time* with each person that reports to you. Find informal ways to create an "open door" policy.

- *Send a colleague*, friend or family member a "get well soon" or "thinking of you" card and brighten their day.

- *Provide honest feedback* and observations to help others grow.

# Courage

*Courageous people believe in doing the right thing for the right reasons even in the face of obstacles and adversity.*

*They don't allow fear to paralyze them from moving ahead and they consistently take small steps forward to complete their goals.*

*With the spirit of tenacity, a courageous person takes risks in order to grow and strengthen their character.*

Courage — step through fear to do what is right

You can't go back, just forward

"Let go!" yelled Carlos, the jumpmaster.

"No!" I hollered back. "I can't do it."

"Now, or you'll miss the drop site. You're making the plane unbalanced." I had no doubt the pilot was struggling to keep my hundred-odd extra pounds, which was hanging onto his wing, from tipping the plane over. Three-quarters of my body was stretched across sky while my right hand firmly clutched the plane wing and my right foot was planted on the wheel. With eighty-mile-an-hour winds pushing me backwards, and 3,000 feet between me and the ground, letting go didn't feel like the best option at that moment, and no, I didn't really care if the plane and everyone in it were coming down with me. I wasn't letting go, and he couldn't make me.

That's when my jumpmaster yelled at me, using words that still ring in my ears nineteen years later. Words that allowed me to effortlessly let go. "Jump!" yelled Carlos. "You can't come back!" He was so right. I couldn't go back, not inside the plane or back to my risk-free life. I needed to make a statement, to let go and take a colossal risk. His words were a metaphor for my life. So I let go, formed a perfect spread-eagle in the sky just like I'd been trained to do, and started to float with ease through the clouds.

"1-1,000, 2-1,000, 3-1,000," I counted. I assumed that at "10-1,000" the parachute would open just like Carlos had told us it would and guide me gently and safely to the ground. But I found myself continuing to count with dedication "13-1,000, 15-1,000," while reminding myself that perhaps I was counting too fast. Stories of people facing death moved through my mind, how they saw their lives flash quietly before their eyes. Unless you have been caught in that precise moment, it is hard to understand. Unfortunately, I now understand the meaning of that expression.

I was conscious of my chute not deploying, conscious of my life up to this point, and of my son, Steven. I was surprised how peaceful I felt. As I fell toward the ground at 1,000 feet a minute, I also remembered blunt instructions from our training drills. "Don't pull your emergency chute too quickly if the main one isn't opening. If they both open up, they will tangle and you won't have a hope. But don't worry, it won't happen; we haven't had an accident in over fifteen years."

I was now thinking to myself that I was in the midst of breaking this stellar fifteen-year record. "18-1,000, 19-1,000 . . ." With great apprehension, I placed my hand on the emergency rip cord, fully prepared to pull it down, when I thought I heard the sound of the main chute struggling to break free from the canvas bag that held it hostage. Do I take a chance and wait for it to deploy? What if it doesn't and I don't pull the emergency cord in time? What if it does and I pull the emergency cord and they tangle into one another? The ground was moving toward me at a rapid pace, so I trusted the gut-wrenching feeling in my stomach and released my grip on the emergency cord. I took a deep, defining breath and waited. In a moment that seemed like an hour, I saw the main chute open. I took another deep breath and enjoyed the view from my vantage point in the sky.

Funny things happen when you free-fall at 1,000 feet a minute with a delayed parachute, picking up speed as you drop. Inevitably, you must hit the earth, and something has to absorb the extra impact. Unfortunately, it was my body. The results: a triple-fractured pelvis, among other injuries — one month in the hospital, three and a half months off work, and years of physiotherapy and chiropractic treatments. If you asked me whether if I would do it again, I would emphatically answer, yes!

If you have every watched the movie *The Princess Diaries*, you might remember these poetic lines: "Courage is not the absence of fear but rather the judgment that something else is more important than fear. The brave may not live forever, but the cautious do not live at all. From now on you'll be traveling the road between who you think you are and who you can be — the two keys to allow you to make the journey."

## Never underestimate your ability to influence change

"Life expands or shrinks in direct proportion to one's courage" was the philosophy of avant-garde novelist Anaïs Nin. It's a stimulating quote because it is so visual. Read it again and repeat it aloud, this time saying it slowly in reference to yourself. "*My* life shrinks or expands in direct proportion to *my* courage." Most of us think of ourselves as not exceptionally courageous, because we have convinced ourselves that we are not the Rex Weylers of the world.

Rex Weyler, a co-founder of the world environmental organization Greenpeace, and his team made the front cover of *National Geographic* with the famous photo of their little motorboat wedged between the defenseless whales and a Russian whaling vessel. The maneuver stemmed from their mandate to protect endangered species at any cost, even at the price of their own lives. If you ask Weyler about this event, he will tell you very humbly that he didn't think he was being courageous at the time; bravery wasn't his motive. He was simply doing what he thought was right, with little regard for his own safety in the moment.

Perhaps we regard ourselves as uncourageous because we're not a young twenty-one-year-old like Terry Fox. In 1979, Fox set out to raise $1 million for cancer research by running across Canada on one good leg and one prosthetic leg. The disease beat him to the finish line and he was forced to stop his run, but not before the world took notice and contributed over $24 million to cancer research. Fox died of cancer in 1981, but his legacy lives on in the more than sixty countries that host the Terry Fox Run annually. To date, the collective courage of thousands has raised over $360 million for cancer research.

Perhaps we don't believe we are capable of being Dr. Mansukh Patel, author, scientist and world humanitarian sometimes referred to as the new Gandhi. Patel was the initiator of the World Peace Flame now permanently housed at the USA. National Civil Rights Museum in Tennessee. This gentle little flame was lit simultaneously by seven different nations. Here's how Patel explains the flames' symbolism: "Greatness comes from the smallest of beginnings, but leaves a large influence." To date he has delivered oil-burning lanterns lit from the original flame to the Pope and to world politicians, reminding them that we all are responsible for creating positive change in the world.

## Everyone has the ability to be courageous

Courage is not necessarily about saving the world in ways that will make the six o'clock news. Every hour of every day we find examples of individuals who exhibit courage in a multitude of ways. Although some are modest, all are important. Booker T. Washington has said, "If you've already made up your mind to do your best today, you will automatically need courage."

For the young bride whose in-laws suddenly moved in with her and started to physically abuse her, arriving for work on time took immense courage. For the father of a severely disabled child who required twenty-four-hour daycare, and who had to get up every two hours to lovingly attend to her needs, courage is an understatement. Contemplate the student holding down three jobs to pay for her education, the single mother of two trying to make ends meet each month, the teller who volunteers for the United Way campaign and raises $1,000 or the assistant manager who just applied for a promotion, got it, and gets up every day to do the very best he can with what he knows, despite his fear of failure.

Courage falls somewhere between the "can's" and "cannot's," stuck between stop and go, sandwiched between powerless and empowered, flanked by yes and no. It is the invisible line between these two polarities that separates us from having fear and becoming fear-less. I believe that the word "courage" is in between any number of these two words; it is what compels us gently and sometimes not so gently from "no" to "on," and then onwards. "On," after all is just "no" spelled backwards. Mark Twain commented that courage isn't the absence of fear, but taking action in spite of fear. This is the test of true courage.

## "NO" is "ON" spelled backwards

As leaders, we must guard against this fine line between no and on, a line not even vaguely straight, and which balances vicariously between *discouragement* and *encouragement*. Courage is a word we must cultivate within our teams. We do so by encouraging individuals to take more risks. They need to be ready, willing and able to step into the unknown — and yes, in some cases, to experience healthy and constructive fear. David Reynolds, author of *Constructive Living,* suggests that we not allow our fears to take up too much space within our lives. Otherwise, we might develop what he calls "chronic fear syndrome." Reynolds urges us to take more risks because it enhances our ability to deal with fear. I have seen far too many individuals and intact teams paralyzed over the years due to suffering from chronic discouragement. This in turn has the side effect of making us overly cautious, rendering us both unable and unwilling to take a chance on being innovative and creative. If we lose these two skills, we lose with them our ability to achieve outstanding results.

Our workplaces require more individuals willing to become leaders, guides and mentors, individuals who take the lead to champion the cause for what is ethical and right. After all, it takes courage to be curious and to explore the possibility of change. One easy place to start is reviewing policies and procedures within our own departments to see how long some of them have been on the books, gathering dust. We need to find out when they were brought up to date. We may even consider eliminating old procedures or policies that no longer serve us. Effective change occurs in incremental steps, which is good because it gives us time to adapt more slowly.

Here are a few discoveries you can enact with yourself and your team to begin to move forward. To practice being more courageous, start by being curious.

- Discover one area that intrigues your mind and makes you want to probe further.
- Discover one area that could use some additional creativity to improve it.
- Discover one question that implores you to find the answer to it.
- Discover one new piece of information you didn't know before.

## We all have a roller coaster to ride

Riding a roller coaster is a bit like skydiving; you hold on for dear life, you get an adrenaline rush, and without doubt, you get a personal growth experience. All three were in place for a friend and colleague of mine who gained valuable life lessons on a fearsome roller coaster ride. Felicia is a great example of turning a *no* into an *on* by reframing her fear and turning it around with courage. I have shared her story many times in keynote presentations. I always show a picture of her at the young age of fifty-six, perched at the top of a sixty-foot pole with only enough room for her two size-six feet and her arms spread wide open to the sunshine.

Felecia was on a five-day Anthony Robbins retreat in Hawaii, where she was the last one still standing at the bottom of a pole that conference attendees were to climb as part of an exercise. She kept mentally preparing to climb to the top as her classmates cheered her on. It was a huge endeavor for my dear friend, a woman who says of her life, "I was fearful of everything — of death, of my children not having a mother. I was fearful their entire lives for their safety and health, that people would talk, what they thought of me. It governed every aspect of my life." Climbing a sixty-foot pole was the starting point on her way to confronting some of those fears, the gremlins that had paralyzed her for most of her life. She finally made it, of course.

Then at the ripe young age of sixty-one, Felicia challenged herself again by taking up an activity that had haunted her for her entire married life. Felecia's husband loved roller coasters, and whenever he had an opportunity, he would ride the exhilarating serpent waves of ups and downs. Felicia always refused to join him, because the idea of voluntarily climbing into a small seat and hanging on for all she was worth was inconceivable. In their thirty-five years of marriage, they never shared this experience as a couple. On a recent trip to Disneyland, she decided she would no longer allow this fear to affect her, so she mustered up all of her courage, bought a ticket and joined her husband in the experience of her life. Felicia later told me with zeal, "I had no idea what I was so afraid of; it was fun! I can't believe I waited so long to ride a roller coaster!" She continues to do so to this day, totally unafraid.

One day, a colleague of mine who is a senior logistics manager — and one I didn't perceive as being afraid of anything — confided to me that he was afraid of roller coasters. It was time, he decided, to face his fear head on. It was time to tame the beast. So one weekend he took his kids to the park and rode the infamous roller coaster. Still scared after the first ride, he wanted to jump off as soon as it came to a screeching halt. But Colin refused to get off until he had moved past his fear. Ten consecutive rides later — yes, ten — he proudly walked away from what he had feared.

## Riding your roller coaster

**Take a moment and name to few fears that stop you from getting on the ride to success, personally and professionally.**

_____

_____

_____

**What is the one roller coaster that you need most to ride?**

_____

_____

_____

**What work-related roller coaster is impeding your team and you from moving forward as a successful group?**

_____

_____

_____

*An invincible dragon guards the entrance*
*It calls itself fear*
*No one knight can defeat it*
*It cannot be slain by might*
*It cannot be convinced to step aside by logic*
*Nor can it be bribed by all the gold of the world*
*It only obeys the heart that it protects*
*And will only step aside if you command it to*

—ROGER BENDLE

## A call to action

In order to grow the character-building trait of courage, and based on what I have learned about myself, I can support a healthier and kinder workplace if I . . .

**Stop** doing:

_____
_____
_____
_____

**Start** doing:

_____
_____
_____
_____

**Sustain** doing:

_____
_____
_____
_____

*"Courage doesn't always roar.*
*Sometimes courage is the quiet voice*
*at the end of the day saying,*
*I will try again tomorrow."*

—MARY ANNE RADMACHER

## Continuous learning suggestions

Ways to express the character-building trait of courage in your life and work include the following:

♦ **Write down four** to five safe risks you would like to take in your work and personal life and then build a plan around each one to get you started.

♦ **Do something crazy** today to step outside of your comfort zone.

♦ **Ask yourself:** What would I do if I could not fail? and brainstorm everything you can think of.

♦ **Refuse** to say "We have always done it this way" ever again.

♦ **Walk a mile** is someone else's shoes: pick up a book or listen to a CD about individuals who have taken courageous actions in their lives.

♦ **Refuse to buy** into the attitude that there is such a thing as failure. Reframe it as the belief that failure represents only growth and learning what not to do next time.

♦ **Ask a colleague** or friend to teach you something that will make you stretch.

♦ **Name three** NO's in your life you want to turn into ON's and get going.

♦ **Interview someone** you know who has been courageous, and get suggestions on how they cultivated their courage.

♦ **Do something each day** that feels like a bit of a stretch toward your goals.

♦ **Step up to the plate** by approaching your manager and asking for a mid-year review of your performance. Ask for positive and constructive feedback.

# Friendship

*A friend is someone with whom you can talk freely, in an open and authentic manner.*

*A friend accepts you without judgment, tells you when you are off base and warmly brings you back to earth with their profound bluntness.*

*Friends give us a sense of belonging and help pull us through during the day-to-day challenges of work and life.*

## Friendship — welcome others into your circle

## There's a little Charlie Brown in all of us

If you're anything like me, you grew up reading the comic strip *Peanuts*. The strip's main character, Charlie Brown, of course, is actually Charles Schulz, a gifted cartoonist who was writing about some of his own cheerless life experiences. Schulz once told reporters that he always felt underestimated by the main influencers in his life — his teachers, coaches and even those he considered to be his peers. He didn't grow up feeling that he was given credit for his artwork, or anything else for that matter. Schulz was a man weighed down by depression, nervousness and feelings of worthlessness most of his life. Most of us have identified with the beloved Charlie Brown at times in our lives, perhaps because there is a little bit of him in all of us.

Throughout my career I have supported the learning and development of thousands of individuals as a facilitator, trainer and human resources professional. When you stand at the front of a room full of people, observing body language, voice tone and the messages behind their words, you become acutely aware of human behavior. I've concluded that we are all susceptible to feeling vulnerable and fragile, regardless of our position or pay. We all lack confidence and a sense of worth at different stages in our lives. We are neither an island nor untouched by this bucketful of human traits and vulnerabilities.

## Gaining a "greatest gifts" mentality

Leaders enjoy the significant power of serving as mentors. We guide human potential and foster self-confidence for individuals under our attention. This power runs on a continuum from powerful to powerless, if not used effectively. If we make people feel mediocre, incompetent, obtuse or lacking in creativity, they will fulfill our expectations. Our perception is our reality, right or wrong. On the other hand, the greatest gift we can give our people is to tell them that they are creative, intelligent, exceptional and possess the ability for unlimited possibilities. Watch them thrive and excel with that! I have yet to be disappointed when I apply what I call the "greatest gift" mentality to my work and theirs. We have no right as leaders to take our mentorship responsibility lightly, nor to underestimate the enormous impact we have as mentors to those around us.

In the case of Schulz, only in his fifties did he begin to appreciate how gifted he was as an artist. That's when he started to route his painful memories into a creative channel, which in turn improved his self-worth and confidence.

## The duty to accommodate self-worth

Never underestimate the importance of mentor-style influences in people's lives; it can compel us toward greatness. In the world of employment law and workers' disability compensation, we live with a term called "due diligence." This is really about ensuring that we've made all efforts to ensure employers meet no legal ramifications. Wouldn't it be a great day in the corporate realm if laws ensured that this same due diligence applied to our role as mentors and leaders — the duty to accommodate self-worth and self-confidence in all our staff?

To test my theory of the impact and influence of mentors, I would like you to think about a few people in your life who have had a positive impact on you, and what difference they made in your way of being. Write down their names and keep writing until you run out of names and impacts.

Here are a few suggestions to get you started:

- An influential teacher who encouraged your development
- A strong mentor who inspired you to reach your potential
- A sincere friend who was there for you during a troubling time or to experience joy with you
- A coach who pushed you in sports to excel or improve a natural talent

Teams participating in this exercise rarely mention presidents and prime ministers, Academy Award–winning actors, sports celebrities or the most recent reality television show winner. They do mention the people who have been heroes in making a difference in their lives. It is not about the rich and famous, because the applause eventually dies down there; the star with the most awards doesn't win in the end. It is more about what Ralph Waldo Emerson said regarding the value of friendships and support: "A friend is a person that I may be sincere before, where I may think out loud." In moving toward a more humanistic approach in the workplace, perhaps we can start by lifting up the little Charlie Brown in all of us.

## Building on a solid foundation of friendship

I have worked with a colourful multitude of teams during my twenty-something years in the corporate world. Some teams I inherited; others I built from the ground up. In this latter case, most of the team came intact when I was recruited into the financial world, about which I knew little. What I did know was the reason I was hired: to make sure a number of serious human resources issues were resolved as quickly as possible, and to do whatever it took to ensure the team was on board. We had our hands full — a small number of branches had just certified into a large union, mainly a self-inflicted cost from managers not listening to staff concerns or responding with a high enough sense of urgency. We were plagued by high disability and stress claims, including two years of declining employee opinion surveys and high turnover, all of which were symptoms of declining morale within the region.

Change had to be swift and organized, but in order for it to occur rapidly, the human resources team had to be given a firm hand in guiding the process. Unfortunately, they faced the disruption of myself as their new leader bringing in a new way of doing business. New teammates entering the group dynamic caused even more chaos. If ever there was a group to observe in the Tuckman model of how teams form, this was it. Bruce Tuckman, an educational psychologist, posed the provocative question "Do teams move through a predicable pattern?" His model is a graceful and supportive explanation of how teams develop and behave during various stages of growth. His research is still as robust today as it was when he created the model back in 1965. Tuckman confirmed that teams move through four stages, namely forming, storming, norming and performing. With great predictability our new team manoeuvred through all four and then we hit the road running and eventually outperformed.

Within one year, we had decertified each of the branches before they negotiated their first collective agreement. We started to see a decline of claims, an increase in disability managment, created a wellness program, brought the employee satisfaction survey up to the national standard, and we commenced on the road to outstanding results over the next three years. When I look back on three remarkable years with this extraordinary team, I reflect on the recipe for success in hopes of duplicating it. One characteristic stands out: the bonds of friendship.

What made this team unique was the presence of a strong intact group, led by friendship long before I got there. It remained long after I left. More than six years later, the team still gets together once a year to celebrate special events in each other's lives — despite the fact that by now all but one have left the organization and moved on to become wonderfully successful in various fields. When you go through rapid change and transition together, there is inevitable fallout in the form of voluntary and involuntary turnover. And, trust me, we had our moments. Yet the prevailing strength that made it work under intense pressure was this underlying bond of friendship, which supported each player through some very stressful moments. Thank you Audrey, David, June, Karen, Leanne, Lynn,

Raquel, Roberta and Sheila for walking the exemplary path of the power of friendship. You have each been great teachers to me.

## The bonds of friendship

One of the most message-charged stories ever told to me involved two friends who were walking through the desert on a gruelling journey to reach an oasis. At one point in the crippling heat, the two friends had an argument. One friend flew off the handle and tore into his walking partner, verbally degrading him. He then proceeded to stomp like an angry child around the desert, yelling in a loud voice at his friend. The friend who was being degraded and yelled at was very hurt by this outburst, which he didn't understand. Without saying a word to his verbal assailant, he picked up a stick lying on the ground and wrote these words in the sand: "Today my good friend Samuel was angry, yelled at me and hurt my feelings."

As the two men continued to walk through the blazing heat, hours later they finally saw an oasis in the distance. They walked until they found water, and here they decided to take a bath in the warm pool. The friend who had been yelled at got stuck in the mire and started drowning, but his friend saved him. After he recovered from the near drowning, he took his knife and carved into a large stone: "Today my friend saved my life."

The friend who had yelled at him and saved his life all in one day asked him with great curiosity, "In the desert after I was angry with you, I yelled at you and hurt your feelings, you wrote this in the sand, and now I have saved your life and you carved it into a stone. Please tell me why." The other friend quietly replied, "When someone hurts us, we should write it down in sand, where winds of forgiveness can erase it. But when someone does something good for us, we must engrave it in stone, where no wind can ever erase it, and we will remember it always."

## Sacred friendships

I am assuming that no one reading this book is unaware of the atrocities committed toward the Tibetan people. Threaded through many of the Dalai Lama books is the theme of forgiveness — his refusal to judge or condemn those who put so many of his people in harm's way. In numerous instances, he refers to what most of us would call a perpetrator or enemy as his "sacred friends." Buddhist principles teach us that it is through pain and adversity that we learn the most, and in this case, compassion and friendship are the teachers.

The workplace is its own potential battleground, full of pain and adversity. Through it we can all learn lessons or explore the depths of "sacred friendships." We can discover the need to reach out with compassion during moments when we're least inclined toward kindness. As the Dalai Lama teaches us, our prime objective and purpose is to help other people. As he puts it, "If you can't help them, then at least don't hurt them."

## Practicing gratitude at work

Saying a straightforward thank you in the workplace isn't as easy as it sounds, yet we know it brings with it great rewards of appreciation, reduced stress and increased performance. Ken Blanchard in his classic *The One Minute Manager* has the most effective yet simple formula I have discovered for getting appreciation right. His recipe is five parts praise to one part reprimand. Kristina Sisu, both a colleague in the health and wellness field and a very dear friend of mine, is the author of the insightful book *Food and the Emotional Connection*. Kristina, a remarkable woman, practices gratitude daily by writing in a journal she carries everywhere with her. Whenever given an opportunity — in an airport, hotel room, waiting for an appointment or doing daily routines — she will stop and write down that for which she is grateful.

Kristina is grateful for the clerk in a store who smiled warmly at her, a sunny day that allowed her to enjoy the ride to her office, a new learning experience, an insightful passage in a book, a healthy meal with friends and her clients. Kristina doesn't look for big things to be grateful for; she sees all the items on her list as equally important. Thanks to her journal, she sees life through optimistic eyes. Her message: if we focus our attention on the workday's modest gifts each day, it will hamper the niggling negatives that distract us from the core purpose of what we do — the tasks that can make a difference. Gratitude would then find a pathway to our workstations and help us create more enthusiasm, optimism and joy in our work, thus helping to dispel whatever makes us angry, frustrated and pessimistic.

"Gratitude unlocks the fullness of life," author Melody Beattie tell us. "It turns what we have into enough, and more. It turns denial into acceptance, chaos into order, confusion to clarity. It can turn a meal into a feast, a house into a home, a stranger into a friend. Gratitude makes sense of our past, brings peace for today, and creates a vision of tomorrow." Gratitude teaches us to reframe and balance the positives with the challenges in our work and lives. Finding a little more appreciation and acknowledgment of what we are doing right instead of accenting what we do wrong can only serve our teams and organizations to create more of this "extraordinary vision for tomorrow".

## Paying kindness forward

Another colleague of mine, Mari-Lyn Hudson, has been actively involved in the kindness movement for years. She created a gratitude journal to build collegial relationships, aptly named *The Workplace Kindness Diary*. This little gem of a book, when passed from colleague to colleague, inspires random acts of kindness. The diary requests up to ten recipients of kindness to record how the act of kindness they received impacted them. They are then urged to commit an act of kindness toward another colleague, who then records how it impacted them — a kind of pay-it-forward process. Something so simple can have an enormous effect, from benefiting an individual to changing the energy of a department.

## Honoring mistakes with gratitude

Amy Dauphinee, who for some time wrote a national newspaper column called "Be Kind," used to gather heart-warming stories from readers, then share them. One that she has allowed me to share involves a young woman working in a busy wilderness adventure company as an office manager.

Jenny was finally beginning to feel comfortable in her position after three months, and was putting in long hours organizing and running the growing business. It was around this time that an act of kindness and compassion in the workplace provided the cement that bonded her to the company. Jenny wasn't sure if she was just tired from working so much overtime, or if it was simply a case of forgetfulness, but one day she made a major slip-up at work. She was scheduled to meet a woman in the afternoon for an informal business meeting in a coffee shop. However, it had been an extremely busy day and the meeting completely slipped her mind. As fate would have it, Jenny's boss Bruce happened to walk into the same coffee shop and encountered the woman waiting for her.

He immediately called her at the office to find out what was going on. Mortified by her mistake, Jenny, as a first reaction, swore on the phone with her boss the other end of the line. Her impulsive profanity only served to increase her distress. Later that day, Bruce walked into the office with a glorious bouquet of spring flowers under his arm. He quietly sat down in a chair across from her and handed them to Jenny. In a voice warm with empathy, he said he'd been quite surprised by her swearing and thought it might indicate that she was extremely upset about her mistake. He gently told her not to be so hard on herself, that making mistakes was just being human. He then proceeded to praise Jenny for her outstanding work and told her how grateful he was that she was part of his company.

Jenny said that his gesture of kindness made her want to work even harder for his company. She believes he taught her an important aspect of respect and appreciation for people in a work environment:

Employees rarely need to be reminded of their mistakes. However, they do need to be told how important and valuable they are.

## Setting people up for success

I would probably never have written this book if not for the unwavering support from my colleague and friend Leslie Nolin-Izzo. This special woman not only encouraged me to complete this book, but also went to great lengths to create a computer graphic for it, so I could use that as a touchstone. If that wasn't enough, she even posted the book cover on the home page of her and her husband's website. Imagine the impetus I felt every time I looked at their site, knowing their clients were seeing the same thing. Talk about an incentive to write! Leslie created and set up an expectation of success for me by placing in front of me the end result I was capable of achieving. Truthfully, she believed more in my ability to write this book than I did, and encouraged me to reach deep into my potential to meet this expectation.

Knowing I couldn't convince Leslie to remove the book cover from the Izzo Group website anytime soon, I decided I'd better give her something to go with the cover. Thank you, Leslie, for being a colleague and friend extraordinaire. I am ever so grateful.

## Practicing friendship at work

*In what one area with a colleague would you like to demonstrate more compassion and friendship?*

_____

_____

_____

*Whom would you like to show more gratitude toward? What would you want to write in stone?*

_____

_____

_____

*Likewise, name one incident you might want to write in the sand — an incident you're ready to let the wind erase, something concerning a colleague that no longer serves any purpose to hold onto.*

_____

_____

_____

*What kind of friend are you at work? What kind of friend would you like to strive to become?*

_____

_____

_____

**Is there someone at work whom you could befriend to make a difference for them?**

_____

_____

_____

**List three people at work to whom you would like to give positive feedback.**

_____

_____

_____

*Your friend is the person who knows all about you,*
*and still likes you.*

—ELBERT HUBBARD

## Showing gratitude through listening

Take a moment to reflect on how you contribute as a friend in the workplace by being a good listener.

- I always show respect for my colleagues' ideas and suggestions.
- I listen more than I talk and don't interrupt, to show I am listening.
- I listen equally to everyone regardless of their position in the company.
- I work hard to not to change the topic when talking to someone.
- I make sincere eye contact with the person with whom I am talking.
- I don't judge or condemn what the other person has to say.
- I realize everyone has an opinion, and I honor where they are at in the moment.
- I am encouraging to those with whom I work.
- I don't assume that I am a good listener because I can hear.
- I am known to be easy to talk to and I keep confidences.
- I don't allow interruptions while talking with others, and I stay present.

## Showing you are listening with your words

Being a friend at work means you show you are supportive and encouraging to colleagues. However, it doesn't mean you support negative behavior if they are being unethical, unkind or not treating others respectfully. Here are some simple yet powerful ways to show you support your colleagues with language that will lift them up.

| Supportive language | Non supportive language |
| --- | --- |
| There are unlimited possibilities out there for you to consider. | Hang in there. |
| You talk about this a lot at work; you must be really upset by it. | Get on with it; it's over. |
| How about we chat over lunch? | I have only a few minutes. |
| I will call you tomorrow if you'd like and we can discuss it. | You know I am here if you want to talk. |
| You must be feeling angry (or sad, upset, hurt). | You have told me that three times now. |
| Tell me how you are doing about not getting the promotion. Is there anything I can do to support you for next time you apply? | Sorry you didn't get the promotion. Its their loss. |

## A call to action

In order to grow the character-building trait of friendship, and based on what I have learned about myself, I can support a healthier and kinder workplace if I . . .

**Stop** doing:

_____

_____

_____

_____

**Start** doing:

_____

_____

_____

_____

**Sustain** doing:

_____

_____

_____

_____

*Don't walk in front of me, I may not follow.*
*Don't walk behind me, I may not lead.*
*Just walk beside me and be my friend.*

—ALBERT CAMUS

## Continuous learning suggestions

Ways to express the character-building trait of friendship in your life and work include the following:

- *Buy a flower a place it on a colleague's desk for no reason.*
- *Walk a colleague to their car or bus stop at night for safety reasons.*
- *Create and celebrate an annual Kindness to Colleagues day/week by committing conscious acts of kindness to each other.*
- *Extend a friendly invite to a shy or new colleague for lunch or to join you on a coffee break.*
- *Offer to switch a shift with a colleague when they need time off.*
- *If someone new has moved into your neighborhood or apartment building, acknowledge this with a little welcome gift and card.*
- *Find ways to continue your friendship outside of working hours.*
- *Place an anonymous supportive note on a colleague's workstation.*
- *Offer to baby-sit for a single mom or dad in your workplace or a couple you know who need a break and time together.*
- *Make a conscious effort to change your language to being supportive and open and caring.*
- *Invite retirees to your next social event.*
- *Practice more positive etiquette at home and at work by committing to saying please and thank you as your everyday language.*
- *Bake a cake for a colleague's birthday and celebrate it as a team.*
- *Strive to be there for others by giving the gift of being an active listener. Stop and pay attention to what people say, and show you are supportive.*
- *Brainstorm with your team five ways to make your workplace more "friendly."*

Chapter Nine

# Kindness in the Community - Sustaining Our Capacity to Thrive

The four character-building traits that support kindness in the community are as follows:

## Service:

*reach out to those around you*

Make a difference in others' lives through giving of one's self altruistically.

## Responsibility:

*take positive action wherever you are*

Identify where you have the power to influence, and accept responsibility for leading positive change.

# Integrity:
*do the right thing*

Generate inclusive conversation around justice, fairness, equality and sustainability.

# Tolerance:
*honor the strength in diversity*

Seek to develop understanding of the intrinsic value of treating everyone equally, with respect and dignity.

# KINDNESS IN THE COMMUNITY
## SELF-ASSESSMENT

Take a moment to reflect on each of the following questions.
Answer each question with a tick if your response is yes.

*yes?*

Do you reduce, reuse and recycle?

Do you volunteer in some capacity in your community?

Do you allow cars to merge into traffic in front of you?

Do you think of local or global issues and their impact?

Do you find a need in your community and champion the cause?

Do you try to be ethical in all your interactions with others?

Do you strive to have socially responsible practices personally and professionally?

Have you ever planted a tree for the planet, with family and friends?

Do you practice tolerance for others less fortunate than yourself?

Do you take responsibility and accountability for leading positive change?

Are you making a difference in the lives of those around you?

*Every man must decide whether he will walk in the light
of creative altruism or in the darkness of destructive selfishness.
This is the judgment. Life's most persistent and urgent question is,
what are you doing for others?*

—MARTIN LUTHER KING JR.

# Service

*When we are in the spirit of service, our intention is to contribute outside of ourselves.*

*Service is about looking around us each day and realizing it's the small acts of service that surround us that make the difference.*

*No act of kindness is too small to make an impact.*

## Service — reach out to those around you

## What are we doing for others?

If you ever have an opportunity to visit the awe-inspiring Martin Luther King Pavilion in Atlanta, I suggest you do so. Dr. King, who died in 1968, has become one the most significant and influential men of our time. Wandering around the bookstore, I came across a little postcard with the following quote from Dr. King: "Every man must decide whether he will walk in the light of creative altruism or the darkness of destructive selfishness. This is the judgment. Life's most persistent and urgent question is, what are you doing for others?"

This is not merely a statement to be taken lightly, but a powerfully reflective question that requires an answer from every individual sharing this world, from the backyard to the boardroom.

- ◆ As a corporation, we need to ask, what are we doing for others that is making a positive difference?
- ◆ As a department, what are we doing?
- ◆ And even more importantly than the first two, as an individual, what am I doing for others?

One morning I happened to be walking by a bank called VanCity Credit Union. Highlighted in the window was a cheerful display of the branch's community contributions for the year. The display pulled me through the doorway, and before leaving, I wrote down one of the comments a staff member had posted on the display board: "Being involved with our communities and staff fundraisers means that coming to work does not mean 'just another day, another dollar.' Instead it's 'another day, another difference.'" This is a true sign of an engaged and committed employee.

## Happy good neighbor day

At the Sidney Florist shop on Vancouver Island, owned and operated by a local citizen, a Happy Good Neighbor Day urges local residents to come and meet new friends. At the community event, the shop gives away six thousand roses. The catch: you have to commit a random act of kindness. Chris Dysart, the shop's owner, says, "Anyone who picks up a half dozen free roses will be asked to sign a promise to keep one of the flowers for themselves and give the others away to five different people, spreading goodwill and friendship in the community to people they know and don't know. We feel it's a great way to give back to the community — one flower at a time!" Of course, all the profits go to a local charity. I excitedly gathered up a friend early and we headed downtown to witness this event. Everywhere we walked, we were enveloped in a sea of beautiful, multicolored roses given out by goodwill ambassadors to others in kindness. Imagine working in the florist shop, how proud you would be.

## Hands, hearts and action

When I helped gather stories for our Kindness to Colleagues campaign, a few in particular stood out. We solicited these stories "from colleagues for colleagues" and encouraged employees to nominate one other for committing random acts of kindness. One story told of how a woman named Linda and her unsuspecting husband unhesitatingly performed a great service for a total stranger. As Linda's colleague wrote, "It was just after we'd had a lot of snow, and an elderly woman was upset because her sidewalk was covered with snow, she had no one to shovel it for her, and she was having a hard time. Linda felt badly for the woman, so she spent the afternoon looking in the phone book and calling around for a senior citizens volunteer organization that could help this woman. Unfortunately, she found none, but she didn't stop there. She called her husband, who happened to be very sick at the time, and asked him to go to this woman's house and shovel her yard for her. So Linda's husband Dan drove twenty minutes to this women's house and shoveled her snow for her. The women was so grateful to Linda and Dan for "taking the time to do such a nice thing for a total stranger."

Another day, another difference. We know we are rising to Dr. King's question, "What are you doing for others?" when our workplace has people who understand that customer service starts not with sales, but with hands, hearts and actions extended first.

## The impact of a kind act is immeasurable

Emanuel Swedenborg, the noted Swedish scientist, philosopher and theologian born in the late 1600s, defined being of service as "an inner desire that makes us want to do good things even if we do not get anything in return. It is the joy of our life to do them. When we do good things from this inner desire, there is kindness in everything we think, say, want and do." What's interesting about kindness is that you never know whom you touch unless they choose to share their experience with you.

Bettina, a colleague of mine, recently recounted with teary eyes her experience of watching a women receive recognition at an awards ceremony where customers nominate employees in the hospitality industry for giving exceptional service. The recipient of the award is an executive housekeeper who works for a national hotel chain. In going beyond her job description one day, she saved a precious life. A hotel guest on vacation from New Zealand had been suffering from depression, even having suicidal thoughts. Bella recognized she was a person in need and took the time to show compassion, friendship and support. The guest later wrote the hotel to say that Bella's humanity helped her make it through a very rough four days before she returned home. We never really know how we can affect lives when we reach out to others in need.

## Man or woman overboard

The ferry's alarm sounded and someone broadcast the announcement, "Man overboard!" The alert crew swiftly moved into action with a sense of focused urgency. The captain of the ferry announced he was going to run a routine rescue drill, using the life rafts to save a man in the water on the starboard side of the ship, if anyone wanted to watch. As luck would have it, I didn't even have to move from my comfortable window seat to witness all the action. I watched in admiration as the crew deployed the life raft. It was only a matter of minutes before the captain announced with pride that the rescue had taken place in record time.

My thoughts turned toward the numerous organizations I have worked for both as an employee and as a consultant. I began reflecting on examples where rescues of an individual involved "all hands on deck." Corporations, I mused, could benefit from a policy for "man or woman overboard" situations. What if department leaders trained staff to come running when a teammate was in trouble — to drop what they were doing, gather around, support them, and lift them back to safety? A little concern and overt compassion up front would surely save many individuals from drowning in feelings of isolation while surrounded by a sea of fellow workers. How little it takes from each person on a team if support rescue operations are well timed, if everyone shares a piece of the extra workload. Together as a team, they could grant a little time off, provide encouraging words, try to listen more. Then, when this person was strong enough, they would be there to lift the next person out of chilly waters.

## So here is some food for thought:

♦ Does your department or organization have a *"man or woman overboard"* approach to supporting one another?

♦ Can you imagine the benefits of forming one? Are you willing to consider it?

As leaders, it's our responsibility to model selfless service by rallying the team when we see a colleague drowning. It is better to toss down the life raft than sit idly by, watching someone we care about sink under the weight of his or her dilemma.

## The five power positions

I believe that leaders go into management for what I have called "the five power positions." Namely, they are attracted by power, prestige, paycheck, personal growth or people. A gifted leader with a service mentality is motivated by their desire to support and grow their people's potential. Such a leader leads people toward a common vision — whereas managers push us to ensure the tasks are completed.

Watch enough leaders in enough organizations, and you will discern three kinds of leaders. One of the more noticeable is the individual consistently in a state of confusion, asking and wondering what just happened. Then there are leaders who carefully watch what is happening around them but don't necessarily take action; they prefer to walk the cautious line. And finally there are the select few leaders who make things happen regardless of the circumstances. It is my hope that we can begin to recruit into our organizations more people with a passion to be of service rather than those who feel they should be served.

Which kind of leader are you? The one who wonders what is happening, the one who watches what is happening or the one who makes things happen?

## Enlightened leadership

It's important to find role models who emulate the core values and beliefs for which we are striving, so we can see that change is possible and feel inspired when unsure whether we are heading down the right path. One progressive leader who makes things happen is Gordon Houston, CEO of Envision Financial, the third largest credit union in Canada and one of the top fifty companies to work for. He caught my attention when he opened a conference presentation by giving his name and position, then announcing with exuberance, "I love my job." If you think those words are unusual coming from a CEO's mouth, take a look at this tagline on every Envision Financial employee's email address: "My promise of enlightenment — I am committed to listening to your needs, understanding your goals and treating you with respect by fulfilling my promises and exceeding your expectations. Always."

Over lunch, I asked Gordon about this unconventional declaration and how it came be. He explained that while going through a merger of two individual credit unions, Envision needed to show employees and customers that management would keep their promises, including a guarantee of no layoffs. The statement evolved from numerous discussions with his team. What I read into this declaration is integrity and ownership, a sense of being of service to fellow colleages and to customers.

It would be wonderfully "enlightening" if each department within an organization took the time to carefully craft a message of service, then broadcast it with as much pride as does Envision Financial. Knowing this is at the bottom of each and every email sent would go a long way to ensuring accountability. It would also serve as a reminder of what true service entails.

## We don't sell dresses, we sell Cinderella

"I tell my staff when they start working for me that when they die, no one is going to *say* 'She sold one thousand dresses.' It's about growing and learning. We don't sell dresses, we sell Cinderella." Gerri Charles is the owner of Champagne and Lace, an incredibly successful wedding and special occasions clothing store servings clients across Canada and the United States.

Gerri and her staff do indeed sell Cinderella. In fact, at times they give it away for free with love. When I interviewed Gerri she shared a memorable story on the power of service. It was a typical Saturday afternoon when an elderly gentleman walked into her store with an eleven-year-old girl in tow. "He was a kind and soft-spoken man," Gerri told me. "He simply said to me, 'This young lady needs a dress. I help out at the local church where her mother is getting married in two hours. She doesn't have a dress to wear to the wedding. Can you help her?' "

That was all the facts Gerri and her team had and all that was necessary for them to move into the instant action of unconditional service. With a flurry of passion and excitement, a number of the staff stepped up without even been asked. Laura asked the little girl how she wanted her hair styled and with bobby pins, ribbons and hairspray flying, a photo-perfect hairstyle was created. Erika went to work on alterations needed on the Cinderella dress the girl picked out herself, while Robynn scooted home to get a sweater that would accent the dress perfectly and keep her warm.

As Gerri put it, "It was like a special project. Customers stopped to watch the action. They were more enthralled with what was happening than with shopping." In the lunchroom Erika recounted that special day, "I have never been prouder to work here."

Karryn emphatically said, "You do it because of people, not dresses. We love each other. There is a sense of community with everyone who works here."

You are so right, Gerri, no one is going to care if you sold one thousand dresses, but they will always remember the day when a little girl that nobody knew was made to feel like Cinderella just for a day.

## The global impact of service locally

A program called Invest in a Kinder World "Coin-spiracy" is a campaign developed for schools and youth groups to raise awareness of how kind acts can create positive messages and initiate change around the globe. Its creators were responding to ever-increasing violence in schools worldwide. The Coin-spiracy program revolves around the launch and tracking of a simple metal coin named UNI — which stands for "the universal nature of kindness." When a school or a youth group pays a small administration fee for a UNI coin, they are instructed to commit three kind acts: one for self, one for the environment, and one for another. From there, the coin is passed forward to the recipient of the kind act, who in turn commits their own three kind acts, and passes it on, much like in the movie *Pay It Forward*. Each UNI coin is coded, thus tracking the kindness adventure through a website.

Now here is the other amazing part of the story. In its two short years, this campaign has generated more than 140 UNI coins around the globe. To date, results include an estimated 100,000 humanitarian acts, over 171,571 hours of service and over $220,000 raised for communities in need, both locally and in forty-five countries. Never underestimate the power of a single idea in the hands of ordinary people with service-oriented hearts.

Our children are our greatest teachers. Perhaps we world-weary adults could take a few lessons from watching their acts of kindness to strangers. How powerful might a similar exercise taken into the workplace be — a UNI coin moving shamelessly amongst departments? I guarantee that we would see the silos fall away, and compassionate friendships rise to the surface.

## Start small and think big

You might have read about Kyle MacDonald in your local newspaper, watched him on television or heard his numerous radio interviews. Kyle is daily becoming a global personality, simply because this young writer did something so innocuous as taking a picture of a simple red paper clip and on July 12, 2005, posted it on his website. He then traded his favorite red paper clip with Rawnie and Corinna for their fish pen, which was exchanged with Annie for a designer doorknob. From Michel came an exchange for a snowmobile, and so which turned into a music contract eventually in July 2006 and a mere 14 trades later, Kyle met his goal of trading up to a house.

When asked in an interview what initially inspired him to do what he is doing, Kyle said, "A game called Bigger or Better. You start with a small object and trade it for a bigger or better object. I make each trade in person, so I usually bring the objects with me in my car or on the plane. I have not spent a cent on the one red paper clip project."

If you talk to Kyle, he won't get as excited about the material objects he traded as much as he got charged about the people he met, their stories, their lives and the many towns he passed through across North America. Kyle says anyone can start their own trading game, but you need two ingredients to be successful. You need to start small and think big. I can't help but hope that his formula is applicable in every aspect of our daily lives. How about if we were to start small and take ten minutes to stop and listen a little deeper to a colleague who needs a friend today. What about reaching out and offering an unconditional helping hand by sharing a bit of someone's workload or offering to drive a buddy home late from work so they don't have to risk their safety waiting at a bus stop? What does it cost to offer a smile of compassion to brighten someone's day, bring them a coffee or offer to be of service in small, meaningful ways by assisting a colleague or neighbour.

I have to agree with Kyle: start small and think big, because the impact of these acts can change a workplace culture and more importantly impact one person's experience for that moment in time, and this is indeed big thinking. I challenge each of us to find our one small workplace red paper clip and, when we do, start trading up and make a big difference.

*My religion is kindness.*

— DALAI LAMA

## How can I be of service?

Vincent Van Gogh was a gifted artist whose experiences with the world were sometimes fraught with confusion and pain. Even so, through his sorrow he called out the words, "How can I be useful, of what service can I be? There is something inside me, what can it be?" Take a moment and ask yourself the same question in regards to your colleagues, department or overall organization.

_____

_____

_____

_____

How can I be useful, and of what service can I be?

Write down as many ideas as occur to you. Go one step further and write down the recipient, then make a goal to commit an act of service in your workplace, local area or even globally.

| *Act of kindness / service* | *Name of recipient* |
|---|---|
| | |
| | |
| | |
| | |

**Name the last four ways you have demonstrated being of service in your work or community, over the past thirty days:**

1. _____
2. _____
3. _____
4. _____

**What has stopped you from being of service in the last twelve months?**

_____

_____

_____

_____

# A call to action

In order to grow the character-building trait of service, and based on what I have learned about myself, I can support a healthier and kinder workplace if I . . .

**Stop** doing:

_____

_____

_____

_____

**Start** doing:

_____

_____

_____

_____

**Sustain** doing:

_____

_____

_____

_____

## Leave a Little Behind

*When you are given a warm, inviting smile*
*Leave a little behind before you walk another mile*

*When you are given a friendly, encouraging lift up*
*Leave a little behind to fill up another's cup*

*When you are given an enthusiastic, 'you can do it, now go'!*
*Leave a little behind knowing you reap what you sow*

*When you are given gifts of kind words, action and praise*
*Leave a little behind to pass along hope and spirits to raise*

*When you are given a helping, generous hand*
*Leave a little behind like footprints in the sand*

*Choose to make a difference in all that you do*
*Remember its simple...Its all up to you*

- OLIVIA MCIVOR

## Continuous learning suggestions

Ways to express the character-building trait of service in your life and work include the following:

- ◆ **_As a team,_** _take a couple of hours to watch one edition of the Extreme Home Make-over TV show. Debrief afterwards and commit to making a difference on a project as a team._

- ◆ **_Instead of a Christmas gift_** _exchange, buy toys for kids and give them to a local charity._

- ◆ **_Gather up_** _all the used eyeglasses from your colleagues and friends, then donate them to a program that benefits those in developing countries._

- ◆ **_Do something special_** _mid-year for the less fortunate and get the whole team involved._

- ◆ **_Gather_** _used professional clothing at work and donate them to a "dress for success" program to support low-income candidates preparing for job interviews or returning to work._

- ◆ **_Watch the movie_** _Pay It Forward and talk about it with your family and friends._

- ◆ **_Join up_** _for a Habitat for Humanity project and donate your time with a group of friends or family._

- ◆ **_Visit an elderly neighbor_** _and bring them flowers or mow their lawn._

- ◆ **_Find a need_** _in your community and champion it by being a volunteer._

- ◆ **_Read to children_** _and adults in literacy programs._

- ◆ **_Take a dog_** _for a walk at your local animal shelter._

- ◆ **_Look around your workplace_** _and reach out to a team member in need of service._

# <u>Responsibility</u>

*Being responsible is a choice we make daily in all our actions and decisions.*

*We are accountable for how we treat others. We know we have the ability to impact and influence those around us, and we always strive to set a positive example for others.*

*We know that everyone on the team is accountable to the group. When it's one person's problem, it's everyone's.*

## Responsibility — take positive action wherever you can

## Judge me by my actions, not my words

"You can be in business, be successful and still be nice," he assures me. "I want people to judge me by my actions not my words," Bob says. Bob Rennie, CEO and founder of Rennie Marketing System, a successful $1/2 Billion real estate business with offices in Vancouver, Washington State and Texas. I asked Bob what he attributes his success to. He humbly stated, "Success is not sustainable without passion for what you do, and you have to be aware of the passion of your people. It's not about the pay, it's about recognition." Here is a gentleman who claims he never told anyone who worked for him to "work hard." He instead believes, "If you give people a sense of power, they will grasp it and run with it."

"It's important," he emphasizes, "to make people feel safe. My team puts me in a safe place every day. They are my foundation. I need to do the same for them." Turnover in his organization is so minimal it's not even worth mentioning, and as an HR professional I welcomed his refreshing twist on what is considered a typical retention strategy, a question human resources asks all the time, namely, *What can we do to make people stay?* Bob believes this is a desperate, fear-based way of thinking and reframes this age-old question with a pragmatic, honest and hard-core question to himself as the leader. *What would make them leave?* he asks, then he attempts to fix it.

I came to our interview with a particular interest in hearing a story recounted, one that had been recently shared with me from a member of his team. It was a narrative that so touched a chord in me that I knew I had to meet the man behind the story and hear it directly from him. The story takes us back four years to a change in business strategy, partnerships, and an adjusting real estate market, a business in transition where budgets were tight. During this time Bob was returning from a business trip to China, where he purchased a gift for each of his staff, brand-name watch knockoffs, a small way of thanking his staff for their hard work. While giving out the gifts at the office, he not only thanked them but apologized at the same time for the watches not being originals and informed them that someday, when the business was more steady, he would replace them with originals. The individual who initially shared the story told me that no one cared if they were originals or not. It was the thought that counted. They knew the business was struggling after the restructuring and this wasn't an issue.

Fast-track to four years later, the business has grown, the team stayed intact, and they meet for cocktails before their annual Christmas dinner. Bob set up a sting operation, luring the team into a local jewellery store where, the staff quickly closed for business except for this unsuspecting group of comrades. Emotions surfaced as Bob once again took them back four years to a promise he had made to them, a promise everyone had long since forgotten, except for Bob Rennie. "I promised each of you when the business was stable again that I would replace those watches with originals. The staff is here to assist you to pick out whatever you would like." The team now has one more thing in common, their new original Rolex watches.

What moved me about this story was what the member of Bob's team who first recounted the story told me. "The watches," he said, "were secondary. They didn't mean as much as Bob keeping his word to us. This meant more to us than the price of any watch."

Perhaps you are thinking about now, "So what? He can more than afford the watches." If so then you missed my point. What is important to note here is the lesson of responsibility, mainly self-responsibility, the keeping of one's word and integrity as a leader. When this particular leader says his philosophy is to be judged by his actions, not his words, I believe he means it. The greatest gift we can give to a team is the feeling of safety in an ever-changing, sometimes tumultuous, unsteady and yes, even at times, an unsafe working environment. Here's a questions for all of us leaders to consider: Do our teams and colleagues feel safe with us? How impeccable are we with our word? Do our words match our actions?

## Remembering to put ourselves in check

We have all had times in our careers when we weren't exactly impeccable with our words, let alone our actions. Where we didn't act as responsibly as perhaps we could have. The key to success is to catch ourselves during or after the act, so we become more responsible for our actions and their impact on others. As leaders, we are all guilty of denying responsibility for our actions, of not championing an issue we could have stepped up to the plate on, of sitting back rather than speaking up against an issue of questionable integrity. Yes, we have acted on our supervisor's "orders" or fallen back on "company policy" rather than working to change a dated approach. It doesn't make it right — it just makes it a learning experience and part of our growth. The message here is to ensure that we keep ourselves in check and continually ask ourselves if there is someone to whom we need to be impeccable with our word. If so, we need to follow Bob's lead.

## We're all responsible to each other

There is a fable of a tiny little mouse that lived on a large farm. One day he saw the farmer and his wife opening a package that had just arrived at their door. The little mouse was horrified to discover that the package contained not a present, but a huge mousetrap. The little mouse ran through the farmyard warning all his friends. "Listen to me, everyone, there's a mousetrap in the house, there's a mousetrap in the house!"

The quiet chicken raised his head and said, "Little mouse, I can tell that you are upset that this big trap is in the house, but truly it is of no concern to me, and I cannot be bothered with it." The little mouse turned to the chubby pig, who said, "I apologize also, little mouse, but this trap is no concern of mine either."

The mouse then turned to the giant bull. "I hear you have a problem, little mouse, but I can't help you either; it's not my problem." The mouse returned to the farmyard house feeling dejected but also realizing he had to be brave and face the trap by himself. That evening, as everyone lay asleep, the sound of the trap catching its prey could be heard throughout the house. It made the farmer's wife jump from her bed and rush to see what was in the trap. In the dark, she could not see that the trap had snapped down on a venomous snake's tail. The snake bit the farmer's wife and she caught a dreadful fever, but the farmer knew how to treat a fever: with chicken soup. So he took his hatchet to the farmyard to get the soup's main ingredient. As the days went by, the wife got sicker, and soon friends were visiting her around the clock. To feed these visitors, the busy farmer butchered the chubby pig. But his wife's health worsened and she died. So many of her family and friends came to her funeral that in order for the farmer to feed everyone, he had to slaughter the giant bull.

This fable has a lot to share with us about the inclusiveness of responsibility. So next time you start to think, "It's not part of my job description," or "It's someone else's problem," know that in truth, if it involves one of our teammates, it needs to become your problem. We are all at jeopardy when a member our group has a dilemma or crisis in their lives. In the course of working together, everyone on a team goes through a calamity of one type or another. If we don't rise to the occasion, they suffer in silence. We need to strive for a philosophy of taking action when we see a teammate asking for our help, of being there to listen and support them before we end up like the farm animals in this fable. If but one of us is at risk, we are all at risk.

## Building responsible teams

A warehouse logistics manager recently tried a leading-edge concept that included empowering his employees to hire their teammates. Now, many of us have been around companies where the staff is one component of the hiring decision. That isn't new or particularly innovative, although it is chic. But this group was different. As frontline workers in a warehouse setting, they had no apparent expertise in hiring. It had always been the role of human resources. More importantly, these employees were not just one component of the hiring decision; they *were* the hiring decision. That made them an empowered team taking full responsibility and accountability for their environment and success.

When I asked how hiring fellow workers made them feel, the responses came fast and without hesitation. "We can make the final decision; it makes us feel important and it's good for moral," one replied. Another piped up right behind her with pride, "We feel empowered and have ownership in our work."

How had this division come to trying the new approach? The leader, Jim, had been juggling turnover for some time, tiring of the swinging door. Then one day he started to listen to the team more closely as they critiqued colleagues serving their first few months of employment. He was astute enough to realize that the team knew exactly which new recruits would make it and which would not. From this pivotal point, he decided to hand over the job to the internal experts, the team itself, ultimately the best judges of character of who would fit into their culture. He began by hand-picking his key staff members, then asking human resources to teach them basic interviewing skills — what to do and not do in an interview. And away they went.

When I joined them one afternoon, they were in the process of interviewing a young man. What an inspiring sight to see seven enthusiastic individuals step outside their traditional roles within the warehouse and take on the responsibility of picking their next teammates. They were slick, organized and had high expectations of the applicant seated in front of them. They held the key as to whether this individual made it to Jim for the final interview; the candidate would first have to make the grade. If he was hired, the warehouse team would also collectively decide if he stayed or went during his three-month probationary period.

Did they take responsibility for going above and beyond the traditional boxed routine job description? Did they accomplish this without hesitation and with stellar attitudes? Did they get the results they wanted to achieve? You bet. When was the last time you heard of a warehouse with less than 20 percent turnover? There is something to be said about the power of responsibility and what you do with it. Jim's advice is to give it away and trust people to fly.

## The responsibility of forgiveness

For two and half years, I ventured into the world of true entrepreneurship by following a lifelong dream to open a specialty bookstore, offering a unique blend of leading-edge business and personal-growth books under the same roof. I learned more in those few years in my 1,600-square-foot store than I learned in twenty years working in senior corporate positions. My most memorable lessons came from my customers — the feisty, forceful, enthusiastic and perplexed individuals who, by the very nature of the store's books, came in search of personal and professional answers. One such individual stands out in my mind as someone who, without ever knowing it, touched my life through her lesson on the importance of forgiveness.

Her name was Lisa. We met one Friday morning while I was working alone in the store. I saw her come in and asked if I could assist her. She replied in a pleasant voice that she had been attending a conference at the hotel beside us and just wanted a few minutes to relax by the fireplace and read. I told her to spend as much time as she wanted to, and to let me know if she needed any assistance. An hour or so went by, and I wandered over to check in politely. That's when I saw her crying quietly in the big green armchair by the fireplace, a book open on her lap. I asked whether she needed a friend or whether she preferred to be left alone. The sad ache in her expression prompted me to pull up a chair beside her. I waited for her to tell me her story.

"How can they possibly forgive him?" she asked me suddenly. "I'm not capable of that. I have too much hate inside of me. It has destroyed my life and my son's." As her story unfolded, I learned that for the last twelve years, this tortured woman had harbored anger and spite for a man who heartlessly murdered her daughter. More tragic, a co-worker was convicted of the crime, a man who had befriended her daughter when she had left home and moved to another town. As we talked and shared tears, she told me how she had encouraged her daughter to move away in order to leave some of her problems behind and get a fresh start in a new environment. Needless to say, she blamed herself for being the one who had pressed her daughter to leave town; now she was gone forever. One life-altering event had left the essence of this mother devastated and aching for internal resolution.

I noted that the book on her lap was called *Soul Stories*, a book of short inspirational stories by Gary Zukav. I probed a little further, curious to see if the book had sparked this surge of emotions for her. Lisa told me the story that had caught her attention was one similar to her own tragic tale. It was a true story about a young native boy who had killed his friend in a rage. Tribal law at the time permitted the band council to decide his fate — whether he would live or die. The band members were torn when the parents of the boy who had been murdered came forward and said that they wanted him to live. They wanted him to live in their son's tepee; they wanted him to wear his clothes, to own their dead son's horse. He was now to be the son who had been taken away from them.

Lisa's story reminded me how the lack of forgiveness can eat us up, can destroy the very precious lives we live, especially if it's accompanied by a lack of self-forgiveness. For years following the tragedy, Lisa was war-torn from endless battles with alcohol addiction, depression and suicide, as well as severe estrangement from her only remaining child. That day in the bookstore, she had been sober going on three years, but the anger and hatred continued to haunt her. She told me it wasn't so much the pain of loss anymore, it was the lack of forgiveness she had bestowed upon herself.

## Forgiveness in the workplace

The need for forgiveness takes many forms in both our personal lives and work environments, but the basics of letting go, of refusing to hold onto resentment, remain the same. The toxic potential of unresolved conversations and conflict in the workplace can be caustic and numbing to the human spirit. We have all witnessed such resentment — holding a grudge against someone else who got the promotion, or against someone who failed to give us a raise or recognition. Then there's perceived or real favoritism, wounds from thoughtless words exchanged during the tension and frustration of not meeting deadlines, and, of course, racism and prejudice.

Dr. Fred Luskin, a professor at Stanford University and author of the groundbreaking book *Forgive for Good*, supports the theory that practicing forgiveness brings with it increased optimism, including improved health and well-being. His research has shown that forgiveness can reduce the effects of depression, hostility, anger and blame. Forgiveness is not only reachable; it is an act that can be accomplished in small increments. We are all capable of forgiving the little bothersome injustices and petty annoyances that occur daily in our workplace. If we choose to, we're also capable of forgiving deeds of a deeper and more profound nature.

In a recent interview, Dr. Luskin stated, "People have the capacity to be more and better and kinder and gentler than they know themselves to be. It is simply a matter of learning and training. Something like forgiveness, something like optimism, something like compassion can be taught. Forgiveness is not esoteric: It is not unavailable: It is not for other people. To me, that is a message of great hope. And I know now, through this research, that we can teach people to become forgiving people. So it is not as much hopefulness as it is passion, guided by the fact that I know it can happen."

## Creating a forgiving community

Luskin recommends that leaders begin by creating a forgiving community within their work environment. We all know what happens when colleagues hold grudges against one another. We have seen the bullying and degrading of character that takes place, regardless of rank and position. Leaders need to be trained how to recognize the festering symptoms, the fallout of not dealing straight-up with the offenders — and the importance of creating codes of conduct to reinforce the importance of letting go.

"Leaders need to model healthy, forgiving ways to respond to frustration and disappointment," Luskin says. "It is very hard to create a forgiveness community if you are harsh and intemperate when people make mistakes, or if the expectations about performance are so high that people don't get both time and privacy to process their own experiences. Forgiveness cannot be only communal; it requires inward reflection. So, you have to have a structure that gives people the capacity to have access to themselves. Companies and families need to provide avenues for people to have their own space. In some companies, you have to run into the bathroom to have a little bit of privacy."

## Creating solutions for forgiveness in the workplace

I recently visited a large financial institution that has taken the proactive approach of setting up a wellness center for employees at their head office to use for "time out." It is a comforting, quiet space, which has been warmly decorated with a couple of recliner chairs, soft lighting, music and motivational books. Staff are actually encouraged to take time — and what is notable here is that is they don't have to wait until their lunch or coffee break to do so. Everyone is encouraged to use the room at their discretion when they feel the need to breathe for a few minutes during the rush of their day. Here they can take ten minutes to calm down and let go of what is upsetting them, so they don't take it out on their colleagues or customers.

## Dr. Luskin strategies to consider:

1. Educate workers about stress management techniques, especially ways to quiet the mind and demonstrate gratitude and appreciation at work.

2. Create an environment where individuals and teams can appreciate the positive attributes in one another.

3. Support individuals when they are upset about issues, and give them time to work through their frustration. Allow people an opening to show their more positive personalities; this helps with the healing.

4. When you need to give feedback, make sure the recipient is open to receiving it. Ask permission to talk; let them choose the timing.

## Workplace etiquette

Emily Post, an American authority on etiquette tells us " Etiquette is the outward manifestation of one's innate character and attitude towards life". As I discuss workplace etiquette I am not referring to table settings or chewing with your mouth closed, rather how to treat one another with respect,  and an honest return to politeness, manners and kindness of words and deeds.

Here are a few suggestions to consider. These go along way in supporting a courteous working environment.

- Discourage all forms of gossip; act swiftly with coaching when it occurs. If it persists, respond as though it's a performance issue.
- Develop workplace etiquette policies to encourage behaviors that exemplify courtesy toward one another.
- Make compassion a corporate value modeled from the top down.
- Expect leaders to admit when they are wrong; this gives others permission to do the same.
- Make saying "I'm sorry" a part of your culture.
- Don't reward conduct that is unethical or unprofessional, regardless of the bottom-line results it achieves.
- Insist managers give credit where credit is due, without exception.
- Involve everyone in the organization in creating a code of conduct and values.
- Don't allow conflict between people to go unresolved; encourage discussion and tolerance for mistakes.
- Teach conflict-resolution skills to everyone from frontline employees to executives.
- Have zero tolerance for hostile, demeaning, blaming and humiliating behaviors toward colleagues.
- Return to 'please" and "thank-you" as an expectation.

*Is there someone in your workplace with whom you need to practice forgiveness?*

_____

_____

_____

_____

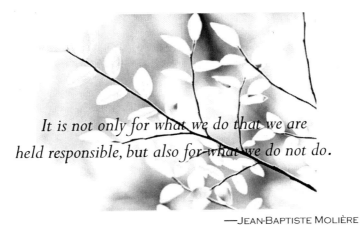

*It is not only for what we do that we are held responsible, but also for what we do not do.*

—JEAN-BAPTISTE MOLIÈRE

## Taking responsibility for our actions

*There is a story about four people named EVERYBODY, SOMEBODY, ANYBODY and NOBODY.*

*There was a very important task that needed to be accomplished and EVERYBODY was sure that SOMEBODY would do it.*

*ANYBODY could have done it but NOBODY did it.*

*SOMEBODY got very angry about this because it was EVERYBODY's job.*

*EVERYBODY thought ANYBODY could do it, but NOBODY realized that EVERYBODY wouldn't do it.*

*It ended up that EVERYBODY blamed SOMEBODY when NOBODY did what ANYBODY could have done.*

-ORIGIN UNKNOWN AND AUTHOR UNKNOWN

| Taking personal responsibility for my actions | True ☑ | False ☑ |
|---|---|---|
| ♦ I never take credit for work others have done. | | |
| ♦ I always take responsibility for my actions even if it means I might get reprimanded. | | |
| ♦ I am always courteous and treat everyone with respect and dignity. | | |
| ♦ I never participate in gossip, and tell those who do to stop. | | |
| ♦ There are no toxic people on my team. | | |
| ♦ We reach out to everyone equally and support one another when a teammate is going through a tough time. | | |
| ♦ I believe that I am responsible for my reaction to what goes on around me. | | |
| ♦ I am the master of my own success. | | |
| ♦ It's my responsibility to manage my own career. | | |
| ♦ I am consistently dependable and reliable at work. | | |
| ♦ If I am upset with the actions of a colleague, I tell them so in a professional and honest manner. | | |
| ♦ I ask for assistance when I need it. | | |
| ♦ If I make a mistake, I believe I own it and have to fix it. | | |
| ♦ When I get upset, it's usually because it's someone else's fault. | | |
| ♦ I would be a happier individual at work if I had a promotion or made more money. | | |

# A call to action

In order to grow the character-building trait of responsibility, and based on what I have learned about myself, I can support a healthier and kinder workplace if I . . .

**Stop** doing:

_____

_____

_____

_____

**Start** doing:

_____

_____

_____

_____

**Sustain** doing:

_____

_____

_____

_____

*Man must cease attributing his problems to his environment, and learn again to exercise his will — his personal responsibility*

ALBERT EINSTEIN

# Continuous learning suggestions

Ways to express the character-building trait of responsibility in your life and work include the following:

- *Share some great positive stories* from your workplace with your family and friends. Let them see what a great place you work at.

- *Share* in the "not so pleasant" work around your workplace. Don't leave such tasks for the "new" employee to take on.

- *Practice setting* an example by opening a door for a colleague, holding an elevator or allowing them to go down the escalator before you.

- *Find two to three ways* to practice taking responsibility for your own actions and behaviours.

- *Review* your life and be honest with yourself when and where you intentionally or unintentionally blamed others rather than being accountable yourself.

- *Commit to giving credit* where credit is due at work. Go back and make amends for any credits due that weren't entirely your doing.

- *Learn to apologize* when need be. Practice saying "I am sorry" and admitting when you have made a mistake. Ask yourself if there is someone at work to whom you own an apology.

- *Write down* the names of individuals you believe you have been holding bad feeling toward. Find ways to let these feeling go, and move on.

- *If you have the capacity in your workload* to take on more responsibility, either temporarily or permanently, inform your manager and help to lessen someone else's workload.

- *Start putting your hand up* and volunteering on committees and contributing to making positive changes in your working environment.

# Integrity

*We know we have integrity when we walk our talk and those who know us can depend on our words and actions.*

*Integrity is taking a stand for what is right and being honest in all our dealings.*

## Integrity — do the right thing

There is a famous quote by John F. Kennedy that never seems to lose its strength with age: "Every time you stand up for an ideal, you send forth a tiny ripple of hope." I keep this quote in a little Plexiglas frame on my desk. I've carried it religiously from office to office for the last dozen years. I do this to remind me in my dark moments, when I feel unsure and discouraged, that what I attempt to stand for can indeed have a huge impact, even if it doesn't quite feel like it at the time.

Like many of us, I am frequently tempted when faced with a decision to take the easier route. I've learned, of course, that doing so sometimes comes with negative consequences, and always results in lessons missed. A friend once told me it's okay to lose, as long as you don't lose the lesson.

## Taking a stand or standing down?

Let me relate a particularly great lesson I once learned, one that to this day exerts a tightness around my heart. In executive management positions, one's role is to see and manage the business from thirty thousand feet: to execute departmental strategy aligned with the overall business strategic plan, to develop your team to become empowered decision-makers and, when required, to step into the day-to-day operations to assist. At the time of this incident, I rarely took away team members' responsibilities because they were so accomplished and passionate about their work, and always operated with a high degree of effectiveness.

However, in this particular case I felt a need for an intervention. My intuition as a human resources professional foresaw what might be a pending dismissal that could result in an attempted suicide. I didn't want the HR advisor or branch manager responsible to have to bear the burden if events took that turn. So, wanting to support the process, I chose to witness the dismissal and use some intervention techniques afterwards. This particular situation was sensitive. A tenured manager had been warned continually of his sexual harassment behavior, among a considerable list of other infractions. Although he had been through many a disciplinary discussion, he continued to show a lack of accountability and responsibility for his actions that finally forced us to take affirmative actions to end our relationship with him professionally. We had all struggled long and hard on this case, because we were concerned about his mental and emotional health.

I drove out to the branch and helped ensure that the manager followed the traditional protocol of dismissal flawlessly. I also spent time alone with the man being dismissed, discussing my concerns for his emotional well-being and recommending the Employee Assistance Program. I left the door open for him to call me and left quietly.

As I drove the thirty-five minutes back to my office, I remember looking at the clock in my car and consciously beginning my seventy-two-hour suicide watch. I was confident I would get a call and sat helpless in my car, feeling alone with what I had just done.

Before I dismiss someone, I ensure that it's a last resort, that every rock has been turned over, due diligence confirmed, and the individual given opportunity to change. My conscience told me that yes, as a team, we had done our homework, and then some, and now it was about an adult who had refused to take responsibility for his behavior. Therefore, change could not occur. The dilemma was whether to protect him from himself or to protect co-workers from him. Ethically, it wasn't a hard decision to make. My mind understood the logic of the decision, but my heart was heavy, knowing that my judgment call could be potentially responsible for someone taking his own life.

I returned to my office, shut the door and asked not to be disturbed. I asked myself, who was I to play God with someone's life? I was the one who had to sign off on all dismissals in the region, and I never did so without weighing both the legal and moral issues. I wasn't so sure I could live with him taking his life, but I believed he would probably attempt suicide, not actually complete it. It would be a cry for help, but then, these matters are never predictable.

I struggled with the question of whether I had made the right choice. Could I have done more, and could I carry on with a free conscience? With a burning need to talk to someone who would take a neutral position, I called my friend and executive coach, Andrew. His experience and wisdom helped me understand that ethically, I had to make a judgment call to protect those who felt unsafe in the man's presence. This was my role and responsibility first. Of course, I couldn't take responsibility for his actions.

As I suspected, within the seventy-two-hour countdown, the employee did attempt to take his life, but was unsuccessful. He finally sought the professional counseling he needed to heal past wounds. I continued my career with a renewed sense of understanding when faced with ethical dilemmas: Stand up rather than stand down when the going gets tough. It's true that every time we stand up for an ideal, we send forth a tiny ripple of hope, one person at a time.

## We all face honesty dilemmas daily

The phone rang. I picked it up casually, only to hear a young woman on the other end clearly distraught, crying hysterically. In a broken voice, she tried to inform me that her manager had raped her in the back room of their store. Initially, the story appeared real. We interviewed the manager, the police became involved even though the manager emphatically denied that the episode had transpired in his store. His colleagues tried to be supportive, but many became distant and aloof. His family life became intensely strained, and his stress levels mounted during a six-month investigation of the case. A very astute police officer ascertained that a number of facts didn't add up. Driven to find justice, he eventually discovered that the alleged victim had fabricated the entire event. Why, you might be asking right now, would anyone do this to another person, to her manager and a fellow colleague? The reasoning behind the motive was as tragic as the ordeal; her employment was going to be terminated, she suspected, so she invented the story to stop from being let go.

Here are other incidents I've had to handle: A male senior executive sexually harassed a woman who reported directly to him for over a year. A teller found a way to access an elderly customer's bank account and withdraw large sums of money. A store manager who accessed the bank deposits made over a long weekend went to Las Vegas to gamble the money away. And let's not forget the warehouse worker who was helping himself to expensive perfumes and re-selling them to friends at bargain-basement prices.

I could go on for pages. Some might think all these are minor compared to the Enrons and WorldComs of the world, but integrity starts close to home. It begins with how we conduct ourselves in our work roles and day-to-day lives.

## Cultivating a culture of trust

I doubt very much that dishonesty starts when we walk into our offices or work site, then waits patiently in the parking lot for our return to our personal lives at the end of our shift. Most likely, dishonest behavior impacts both areas of our lives. Integrity is a fundamental attribute of who we are, and we become less effective in the world of work when we compromise this attribute — even where we think it's acceptable to eat the chocolate bar or sandwich while on shift, pocket bits of change, take home the Post-it notes or computer paper.

If we are to combat this issue in the workplace, we have to start talking about the elephant in the middle of the room by searching for solutions, which includes everyone's frank input. Many managers spend far too much time and wasted energy plotting how to catch someone doing something wrong than placing emphasis on catching people doing things right. May I suggest that we need to start by cultivating a culture of trust, by educating on such values as honesty and integrity. We need to return to the simplicity of the Golden Rule — "Do unto others as you would have them do unto you" — and emphasize the significance of keeping our word.

# There is no grey area in integrity

For years, I taught a program on preventing loss at the retail store level. Its premise was to teach managers a proactive approach to preventing employee theft, deterring shoplifting, and putting into place proper procedures for effective paper controls. One of the key concepts was the "eighty twenty" rule: 10 percent of employees will never steal no matter what temptation you put in front of them, another 10 percent will always be dishonest no matter how motivated or careful your controls. The remaining 80 percent, given an opportunity, and if enough carrots are dangled in front of them, will become dishonest. Who really knows if this statistic is sound, but in witnessing the hundreds of managers over the years, I can say that many of the internal losses within an organization are self-inflicted wounds, brought on by employees experiencing a lack of motivation and gratitude.

Do we each really know right from wrong, or can we somehow rationalize our behavior with so many excuses that we need not hold ourselves accountable for our own misconduct? John F. Dodge, who in 1914 with his brother started their own automobile manufacturing company, which later sold to Chrysler, said, "There is no twilight zone of honesty in business. A thing is right or it's wrong. It's black or it's white." Why we fail to hold one another accountable for our conduct through honest feedback is beyond me. I continually ask myself how we have arrived at a place where we have lost communication with those we work alongside daily. So deficient are we are at communication that some of us have taken to writing apologies on a website instead of feeling safe enough to say it to our co-workers.

Jay Rayner, author of a book called *The Apologist*, started that website. Its primary function is to allow individuals a forum to say they are sorry for everything from family issues to work-related conflicts. There is an entire workplace section, which includes one item from a disgruntled employee apologizing for spitting in his manager's coffee when he wasn't looking. Another reads, "Sorry for my dishonesty. I would like to say sorry to my last employer. Over the time I worked for them (eight years), I started to help myself to petty cash. I was never caught, but in the end I left because I felt so guilty. I am sorry for this and just wanted to express it."

My first thought on reading this was what a waste of an excellent employee. My next thought was where was management during those last eight years? Here is an example of the self-inflicted wound. I can't tell you how much time, money and energy has been wasted in organizations engaged in feverishly trying to catch a thief, when such resources would be far better spent motivating, inspiring and listening to the 80 percent working diligently every day, serving customers.

# HOW DOES YOUR INTEGRITY STACK UP?

Take a moment and reflect on each question and how it has applied to your career.

| Place a checkmark beside those that ring true to you. | ☑ |
|---|---|
| I scan the Internet at work to research information for my personal use. | |
| I have witnessed my colleagues stealing company property such as food items, office supplies, etc., but didn't report it or tell them to stop. | |
| I have been known to add illegitimate extras to my expense account. | |
| I come in ten to fifteen minutes late on a consistent basis, but always leave on time. | |
| I have called in sick when I just wanted a day off. | |
| When a co-worker makes racist slurs about a customer or colleague, I just keep quiet. | |
| I have treated someone with favoritism because they were my friend, not because they were the best person for the job. | |
| I have lied to my direct report so I wouldn't get into trouble. | |
| I know a colleague is being dishonest handling cash, but I haven't said anything to anybody. | |
| I have made long-distance phone calls while at work that were not work related in any way. | |
| I have lied to a client just to make a sale. | |
| I have inflated my resume and lied about my skills during a job interview. | |
| I am not always honest with my customers. | |
| I have witnessed unsafe procedures in our workplace but keep quiet. | |
| I have seen co-workers treated disrespectfully, bullied or harassed by other colleagues, but I don't get involved. | |

## The Constant Companion

*I am your constant companion.*
*I am your greatest helper and heaviest burden.*
*I will push you onward or drag you down to failure.*
*Half the things you do, you might just as well turn over to me and I will be able to do them*
*quickly and correctly.*
*I am easily managed — you must merely be firm with me.*
*Show me exactly how you want something done and after a few lessons,*
*I will do it automatically.*
*I am the servant of all great men and women;*
*and alas, of all failures as well.*
*Those who are great, I have made great.*
*Those who are failures, I have made failures.*
*I am not a machine, though I work with all the precision of a machine*
*plus the intelligence of a woman or a man.*
*You may run me for profit or for ruin — it makes no difference to me.*
*Take me, train me, be firm with me, and*
*I will place the world at your feet.*
*Be easy with me and I will destroy you.*

*WHO AM I? I AM YOUR HABITS.*

—AUTHOR UNKNOWN

**Name two habits you would like to eliminate from your personal life that no longer serve you.**
1. _____
2. _____

**Name two habits at work you would like to eliminate that no longer serve you.**
1. _____
2. _____

## A call to action

In order to grow the character-building trait of integrity, and based on what I have learned about myself, I can support a healthier and kinder workplace if I . . .

**Stop** doing:

_____

_____

_____

_____

**Start** doing:

_____

_____

_____

_____

**Sustain** doing:

_____

_____

_____

_____

*Hold yourself responsible for a higher standard*
*than anyone else expects of you.*

—HENRY WARD BEECHER

## Continuous learning suggestions

Ways to express the character-building trait of integrity in your life and work include the following:

- **_Ask yourself_** if there is anything you have taken home from work that is company property and if so, then return it.

- **_Write a list_** of people at work that you may have offended with your words or actions and find a way to redeem yourself either through an apology or a kind act toward them.

- **_Attend a course_** on ethics in the workplace and then share the information with your team. Make a point of discussing ethical business practices at least once a quarter.

- **_Take a stand_** and do what is right by refusing to participate in any unethical behavior by yourself or with your colleagues/friends, regardless of how insignificant you think it is.

- **_List four to five habits_** you have developed over the years that are stopping your progress at work and in your life. Ask your colleagues to support you in breaking them and then find ways to celebrate when you do.

- **_Strike an agreement_** with yourself that you won't call in sick at work unless you really are. Strive to honestly express yourself and tell your manager you need a day off and for what reasons.

- **_Review_** how your integrity stacks up on the quiz and pick two areas you want to improve on as of Monday morning.

- **_Take a stand_** on an integrity issue in your work or personal life & then watch yourself grow

- **_Refuse to claim_** anything on an expense report that isn't true.

# Tolerance

*Our workplaces and neighborhoods are made up of a diverse mixture of multicultural, multigenerational and multidimensional people with different beliefs, wants and needs.*

*Each person and business has a story to tell of struggles and triumphs that need to be shared openly.*

*By opening ourselves up to welcoming others into our circle of friendship, we break down the barriers that cause fear and hurt.*

## Tolerance — honor the strength in diversity

Three key areas form the Noble Eightfold Path of the Buddhist tradition: wisdom, ethical conduct and mental development. One of the eight paths is Right Speech, which is very important in the context of Buddhist ethics. The core belief is that our words, including what we say and hear, can make or break our lives. Our words have the ability to help us make and keep friends. They can bring peace or, at worst, create conflict and violence. Right speech, according to the website www.thebigview.com, is:

- ♦ To abstain from false speech, especially from telling deliberate lies and speaking deceitfully
- ♦ To abstain from slanderous speech and from using words maliciously against others
- ♦ To abstain from harsh words that offend or hurt others, and
- ♦ To abstain from idle chatter that lacks purpose or depth — to tell the truth, and speak in a friendly, warm and gentle manner.

## Our words have the ability to inspire

This applies from the schoolyard to the workplace in how we conduct ourselves with our colleagues and friends. With leadership comes the overwhelming ability to tear down or build up. Our words can motivate, inspire and support, or they can reject, humiliate and condemn. This is the very nature of the power imparted with the name on our business cards; it's also the responsibility most often taken for granted. Margaret Wheatley, writer and community advocate, sends a strong message to leaders regarding their employees. She says employees are a blessing, not the problem within our organizations. Wheatley's conviction is that "it's not differences that divide us. It's our judgments about each other that do." Such judgments can destroy working relationships that otherwise have the potential to be joyful and productive. Such judgments can demolish relationships, making them manipulative and toxic.

*"We may all have come on different ships, but we're in the same boat now."*

—MARTIN LUTHER KING JR.

## Friendliness is in; being cruel isn't cool

Landin is a young man who glows with strength and courage in the face of indifference and the cruel intolerance of others toward him. I am not sure how one gets to be so utterly wise at the tender age of sixteen years, but life's lessons have a way of bringing with them the gift of wisdom if one takes the time to see and acknowledge it. This is how Landin sees the world, and it's obvious by how he conducts himself. We met while attending a Train the Trainer program, aimed at creating instructors for a wonderful program called The Virtues Project, a program to teach values and positive traits to children. Everyone was invited before the class to enter a contest by submitting a kindness story, which later we read to the class. Landin's story won first price and he has kindly given me permission to print his story verbatim. There wasn't a dry eye in the room as we watched this brave young man share his story.

He titled it "Friendliness is in; being cruel isn't cool," a profound statement in itself.

> Friendliness is a virtue that I cherish. As early as grade four, I can remember being a shy, lonely person with few genuine friends. There were some students whom I believed to be my friends, even though they didn't want to be seen with me. I felt rejected by my peers. Public school was a nightmare of harassment. Consequently, I believed there was something wrong with me. I thought that I was born different, and would be that way forever. Discouraged, I sought refuge in isolation.
>
> In high school, I was labelled "Beavis," a nickname that spread throughout the school. I cringed whenever I heard it. I was beaten up, had a knife held to my throat, and had my life threatened. Bullying caused me so much pain that I hated school: Nothing seemed worthwhile. I wanted to escape. At home, my father was an adult bully who used an arsenal of verbal, emotional, psychological, physical threats and abuses. I was too scared to say anything about my situation. I tried to endure . . . but it stirred around in my head and traumatized me until I couldn't cry anymore. I became depressed and numb.
>
> Fortunately, at this critical juncture, friendship provided intervention, counseling and protection. Now I'm supported, and learning to defeat my demons. I have respect for myself and my uniqueness. I have ADHD and Tourette's Syndrome, and I am happy to be different. It helps me to be more creative.
>
> Taking a stand can make a difference. It did for me! Be a friend!

Thank you, Landin, for being such a great teacher at such a young age.

## Tolerance starts with one's ability to apologize

"I'm sorry" sounds easy enough, doesn't it? It's only two words. Yet we rarely hear it echo through the hallowed halls of work. Why, exactly, I am not quite sure, and yet every time it is said there is a magical response. Do leaders resist uttering this phrase because of their egos? Or because it shows we are weak and easily taken advantage of? Maybe we think we should exhibit a personality of perfection where leaders don't make mistakes, they make decisions.

For years, I have mediated between individuals: between managers and their staff, between colleagues, and between managers and their leaders. It took me way too long to figure out that closure and learning never fully occurred until each person realized the emotional impact that the event and issue had on them, regardless of how insignificant it was in one person's eyes. So I began encouraging each person to apologize for their perceived conduct to their colleague — conduct that might have been taken by the other person as harmful. I explain that one's perception is one's reality. It doesn't matter what the issue at hand was or who was right or not right; the apology was for hurt feelings, the issue still to be resolved. However, the impact of saying "I am sorry if I hurt your feelings in front of your peers in the lunchroom" goes a tremendously long way in allowing conflict to resolve itself quickly with less residual fallout.

In most cases, the individual realized that they were acting out of frustration when they said or did what they did. It is all too easy to dismiss another's thoughts and feelings, and concentrate only on the facts. But the facts must be weighted with how the other person was made to feel during this time, as well. Getting to the feelings is as important as getting to the facts: By the end of the intervention, each person needs to determine whether they acted with integrity and respect for the other individual in front of them. They must ask themselves if they spoke their truth respectfully or were rude or condemning. Did they take away or undermine their colleague's self-worth?

Building tolerance for one another comes when we move from the norm of common ground to higher ground by being able to apologize. We need to recognize that it isn't necessarily about admitting liability for the situation in question, but more about knowing the other person's self-worth stayed intact in the process.

# Higher ground apologies

These are some key pointers when delivering an apology with a higher ground intention:

◆ Take responsibility for the impact or harm you might have had on this individual by naming and taking ownership of it.

◆ Take your share of the responsibility to preserve the self-worth and dignity of your colleague.

◆ Respond in a timely way — the longer you wait, the less meaning and impact your words hold.

◆ Realize you might not be able to control how the other person accepts your words.

◆ Be honest with yourself about how you might handle this situation differently if given another opportunity.

◆ Ask yourself truthfully if you have a habit of not being able to admit you made an error in judgment (taking credit for others' work; using demeaning, sarcastic and abrasive language; undermining or criticizing others).

◆ Ask yourself why you were so intolerant of this individual's actions. Ask yourself if this is more about you than them.

◆ Admit you might have hurt the feelings of another person with your words or actions and resolve to repair the matter quickly.

◆ Make a point of practicing saying you're sorry so your colleagues will know you are as good as your word and can admit when you have crossed the line.

# We have the potential to turn a life around

Antoine de Saint-Exupéry, author of the famous children's book *The Little Prince*, informs us "It is only with the heart that one can see rightly; what is essential is invisible to the eye." The human spirit is immeasurable to the common eye, yet there is so much that is measurable: There are areas of the physical, mental and emotional self we allow to go unrecognized and unnoticed. In grade eleven, I had an enlightening guidance teacher who taught us the inspirational words of author and teacher Leo Buscaglia. Like clockwork, once a week for one year, we reluctantly allowed our impressionable sixteen-year-old minds to be subjected to viewpoints taken from his first book, which was modestly titled *LOVE*.

While listening to his tapes during class, or reading from his book, our young teacher would encourage us to put our heads down on our desks, close our eyes and listen carefully to what this sage had to tell us about loving others and ourselves. One lesson still stands out in my mind thirty-one years later. It was on being tolerant of one another. She commenced the lesson by writing on the chalkboard the following quote from Buscaglia: "Too often we underestimate the power of a touch, a smile, a kind word, a listening ear, an honest compliment, or the smallest act of caring, all of which have the potential to turn a life around." Obviously, this resonated in my young mind, because I wrote it down and have kept it with me all these years. I fondly think of Landin and many more when I remember this quote and our ability to influence others in a positive way by doing nothing more than reaching out and using the power of our speech and actions.

## I am just one man

It's easy to believe as a lone individual we are not capable of making an impact that will make a significant enough contribution to bother with, so we get discouraged and do nothing much of the time. As humans we truly do underestimate our ability to turn a life around, so if you ever start thinking this way, I want you to think about the simple yet profound influential act of one man named J.T. Thompson. J.T. lives in Key West, Florida, but has made an impact that is quietly moving around the globe.

J.T. says, "I am just one man, doing what I can, but I have decided to do what I can to promote the worldwide understanding of the concept of human unity. Our modern world reminds us daily and incorrectly how separate we all are. From politics to religion to sports and even entertainment, we're told it's *us against them*." J.T. advises each of us to "examine closely the true motives of anyone who tries to tell you it's 'us against them," because the truth is that there is no 'them.' There never was and never will be. There is only us, one human family."

So what did "one man doing what he can" actually do? He designed, printed and has distributed to date over 600,000 bumper stickers around the globe with a straightforward black and white message that simply reads, "All People Are Created Equal Members of One Human Family."

J.T. Thompson gives them away free of charge, and as many as you can use, distribute or even reproduce. The magic of this project is that his only request is that those receiving the stickers do not profit from their distribution. Since the inception of the project with a small number of stickers, the One Human Family motto was proclaimed in 2000 to be the official philosophy of the City of Key West, Florida, and in February 2001 this same motto was endorsed by the Simon Wiesenthal Center for Tolerance in Los Angeles.

Perhaps if we each adopted the motto of "I am one women or man doing the best I can," we could create a spark of local or global magic like our friend in Key West.

## All people are precious

At a retreat for executives a few years ago, Dr. Hugh Drouin, former executive director of Family Services of Ontario and author of *No Stone Unturned*, repeatedly said, "All people are precious." These four words on their own have little force, but when placed together, can become a creed by which to conduct our actions and words. Imagine if this creed became a living, breathing philosophy within our corporate walls and city streets, how the pain would lessen in how we treat one another. There would be no need for courses on creating respectful workplaces, no need for campaigns on diversity and racism, no policies in place for sexual harassment or bullying. It is profoundly simple statements like these that we forget when we are forced up against a wall with deadlines and the daily pressures of life. When we are not sure what to do next, we need to be reminded to think with our heart, be reminded that our work is not just about the quality and quantity of the product and services we sell, but also about the quality of the relationships we forge with one another. Our relationships are made up of precious people.

Speaking of how precious people are, I would like you to take a moment and read through this poem at least twice and note your reaction to it as you read it.

## *Choose to Contribute or Condemn*

*He looked me up and down, a shadow of judgment his eyes did cast,*
*Upon my body, mind and spirit and oh how very long it did last.*

*This judgment, this unspoken opinion in the air,*
*Do you really believe it's honest my friend, and fair?*
*Was it my colour? My creed? My beliefs? I somehow doubt*
*It couldn't possible be, cause of me you know little about.*

*Those glances, those words uttered in front or behind my back,*
*All dispirit, destroy and condemn me, merely because of knowledge you lack.*
*So when you decide I am not good enough to join your circle of friends,*
*First, think of me as a gentle reminder, that judgment always loses in the end.*

*The sender must receive it back; around and around it eternally goes,*
*We each create a circle of love or fear, it always shows.*
*So, go gentle with your words and promise, no harsh emotional imprints to make,*
*Trust me, it only hardens your heart, crushing your spirit in its wake.*

*Each one of us will choose to contribute or condemn,*
*And there will be no in-between road to walk in the end.*
*You must decide of which path to trend upon,*
*A life of judgment that comes back, or a life of acceptance where we all belong.*

-OLIVIA MCIVOR

# Reflect on these questions:

**Think sincerely about it: at work do you have a tendency to contribute or condemn more in general?**

_____

_____

_____

**I notice I have built walls of judgment. It makes me feel...**

_____

_____

_____

**One example of when I contributed was...**

_____

_____

_____

**Areas I need to consider becoming more accepting and tolerant of others include:**

_____

_____

_____

# Contributing to a tolerant work environment

Contribute to a tolerant workplace by refusing to participate in negative comments, gossip and toxic behaviors.

**List the people you gossiped or complained about this week at work.**

_____

_____

_____

*Try to identify the most important issue floating just above the surface that made you strike out in gossip.*

_____

_____

_____

*What did you hope to accomplish by gossiping?*

_____

_____

_____

*List the number of putdowns you have uttered this week.*

_____

_____

_____

*How would it feel if other people were saying these things about you?*

_____

_____

_____

*What do you want to do differently next week regarding being more tolerant of your co-workers?*

_____

_____

_____

*"Commit to leaving your workday more stellar than you started it"*

—OLIVIA MCIVOR

## A call to action

In order to grow the character-building trait of tolerance, and based on what I have learned about myself, I can support a healthier and kinder workplace if I . . .

**Stop** doing:

_____

_____

_____

_____

**Start** doing:

_____

_____

_____

_____

**Sustain** doing:

_____

_____

_____

_____

_Three things in life are important. The first is to be kind,_
_the second is to be kind , the third is to be kind._

—HENRY JAMES

## Continuous learning suggestions

Ways to express the character-building trait of tolerance in your life and work include the following:

- ◆ <u>*Hold an "honoring diversity"*</u> *potluck lunch and have everyone contribute by bringing an ethnic food from their culture. Allow time for each person to explain the significance of the dish.*

- ◆ <u>*Develop a zero tolerance*</u> *in your workplace for any behaviors that could be perceived as prejudiced or disrespectful.*

- ◆ <u>*Create*</u> *a working environment that is inclusive and diverse, and find ways to celebrate everyone's uniqueness. Hire diversity.*

- ◆ <u>*Become curious*</u> *about your colleagues with diverse backgrounds, ask questions and learn as much as you can about their values and beliefs.*

- ◆ <u>*Include diversity*</u> *training in your courses and orientation programs.*

- ◆ <u>*Create guiding principles*</u> *with your teams on how you will treat one another with respect and dignity. Have each department create their own principles.*

- ◆ <u>*Attend cultural events*</u> *with your family and friends.*

- ◆ <u>*Eat in restaurants*</u> *you are unfamiliar with, and delight in culturally rich foods and tastes.*

- ◆ <u>*Read a book*</u> *on a topic or concept you are unfamiliar with to increase your knowledge.*

- ◆ <u>*Adopt a foster child*</u> *from a developing country and watch as they grow up.*

- ◆ <u>*Practice*</u> *nonjudgmental, refuse to gossip.*

- ◆ <u>*Implement a Kindness to Colleagues*</u> *initiative in your workplace.*

The Business of Kindness

Chapter Ten

# Implementing a Kindness Initiative in Your Workplace

## Creating a change of heart initiative

Seed by seed a garden is planted, grain by grain we create a healthy baked loaf of bread, and brick by brick we build magnificent stone cathedrals and names. Change is a process, a work in progress and a labor of love for those we want to impact. John Schaar, an American writer and professor of political philosophy at the University of California, has such a weighty view on change that I feel strongly compelled to share it. "The future," Schaar states, "is not a result of choices among alternative paths offered by the present, but a place that is created — created first in the mind and will, created next in activity. The future is not some place we are going to, but one we are creating. The paths are not to be found, but made, and the activity of making them changes both the maker and the destination."

I will dare to add that it can also change destiny, and our actions control how the paths will lay out. This gives me great hope for our organizations both small and large — knowing that positive change can occur, that it lies within our grasp. As our organizations mature both intellectually and emotionally, we begin to realize that it is not the techniques or tactics of change we require, but a change of heart in how we do business.

# Four reasons to start a success kindness campaign in your organization

This entire book was born of a rather innocuous idea I wrote on a scrap piece of paper in 1999. I originally wrote it in the form of a question: "Would it be possible to hold a 'Kindness to Colleagues' week, and if so, what would it look like?" The original idea and inaugural run of the event was named Kindness to Kolleagues with two Ks, which I thought was rather catchy. Later, as it evolved, I changed it to Colleagues with a C. From the inception of a simple idea, I brought the idea to a dedicated team of individuals called the Healthy Living Committee, devoted to implementing a wellness initiative.

To launch a Kindness to Colleagues campaign, you will require three key components to be successful: 1) a coordinated and 2) an actionable plan that 3) inspires employee buy-in at all levels. This initiative sets itself apart from other initiatives. Here are four reasons to mull over the idea.

### Reason #1:

It provides a comprehensive, coordinated framework for integrating wellness into the corporate fiber of the whole organization. It also provides a rationale and theme to facilitate team building between intact and interdepartmental work groups. A Kindness to Colleagues campaign will integrate a range of other initiatives such as corporate rewards and recognition programs, succession planning, community contribution, environmental responsibility, and corporate social responsibility — all together under one umbrella.

### Reason #2:

The initiative was designed around the theme of kindness specifically because kindness is actionable and easy to understand regardless of language, gender, position or race. It has limitless possibilities for ideas that can be converted into simple action, at all levels of the organization. But the real power of the program is that people can be empowered to commit kind acts in the workplace with little or no instruction at all.

**Reason #3:**

Many wellness programs in organizations have had great success motivating people with incentives ranging from weight loss to relaxation techniques. One notable fact about traditional wellness programs is that they attract only those who are already healthy; they speak loudly to the converted. A Kindness to Colleagues campaign offers a way for individuals across the range of physical health to get involved immediately in small ways to enhance their health and well-being. Although many individuals require huge motivation and incentives to begin an exercise program, they will likely be less averse to "committing" a kind act toward a colleague or themselves. The resulting incremental increases in self-esteem, as well as in support from co-workers, are far more likely to produce an environment where such individuals feel ready and able to take more drastic steps toward bettering their mental, physical and emotional health.

**Reason #4:**

Kindness is a subject that speaks to everyone. It resonates with both the heart and the mind. Rather than trying to motivate individuals, the kindness theme is designed to inspire them to act by resonating with core human values. This shift toward inspiration rather than motivation is ultimately what will make an initiative successful over the long term, and will continue to attract individuals to pursue and maintain greater levels of health, performance and fulfillment at work and in their lives overall.

## Weaving kindness into the corporate fiber

The Kindness to Colleagues initiative was designed to be a proactive approach to enhancing the wellness and sustainability of an organization at a grass roots level. Its prime objective was to counteract any potential there might be for the often hidden, subtle violence in the workplace, and simultaneously facilitate the integration of a broad spectrum of organizational initiatives already in motion.

Below is an example of the kindness umbrella and how each of the traditional programs and initiatives leaders support within their organization can be enhanced and strengthened under each of the three kindness themes. It is just a matter of finding ways to weave a kindness idea into each of these initiatives.

## The Kindness to Colleagues umbrella

What initiatives do you have within your organization that might fall under each of the three themes? Name as many as you can:

**SELF**

- Occupational Health and Safety
- Wellness programs
- Employee Assistant Programs
- Career counseling
- Benefits
- Performance management

**COLLEAGUES**

- Training & development
- Social activities
- Employee surveys
- Diversity programs
- Rewards and recognition
- Anti-harassment programs

**COMMUNITY**

- Volunteering
- Public relations
- Corporate social responsibility
- In-kind contribution
- Donations
- Customer service

Kindness to oneself:

_____

_____

Kindness to colleagues:

_____

_____

Kindness in the community:

_____

_____

## The nine vision questions

Ask yourself:

1. Will I be "ignited" by this vision?
2. Will this vision stand the test of time with my core values, my teams and the organizational values?
3. Will I require support and resources from various levels of management? Who will be advocates and adversaries?
4. Will I be given an opportunity for growth and personal development?
5. Will others be able to catch this vision and be as passionate about it as I am?
6. What are the risks I/we face? What is the worst-case scenario with which I am prepared to live?
7. What rewards would I/we achieve? Intrinsic/extrinsic and does it even matter?
8. What am I prepared to do? How far can I stretch? Can my team stretch?
9. How badly do I want to make a difference on this issue? (rate from -1 to +10)

A custom I've found successful over the last dozen years is to ask myself some imperative questions whenever starting a new strategic plan, project or contract. I have found it particularly important to field these questions in an introspective manner, especially when I'm pushing the envelope or championing an initiative ready to break new ground. Any nontraditional journey can be a bumpy road, full of unsteady moments, especially when you are introducing new concepts and ideas. Think what you could be up against, and whether you have the resolve and commitment before you begin. Gandhi described the process of breaking new ground quite eloquently: "First they laugh at you, then they get impatient, then they get angry and then you win."

Here is what I warmly call my nine vision questions. They have guided me through many a decision in my personal and professional life. Invest in a journal to start with; write down the quest you would like to undertake. Be clear and specific. Then copy each of the following questions in it and take as much time as needed to become intimate with them before answering thoroughly.

## The three distinct stages of implementation

In order to facilitate implementing a Kindness to Colleagues campaign in your workplace, the program has been organized into three distinct stages:

Planting the seeds of kindness in business

Cultivating kindness in business

Harvesting kindness in business

The first step is about getting started, literally planting the seeds of kindness in business. As you gain the support and leadership necessary to foster the next stage of growth, you may choose to proceed to the more involved stages of cultivating and harvesting kindness in business.

## STAGE ONE: planting the seeds of kindness in business

*Kindness is the golden chain*
*by which society is bound together.*

—JOHAN WOLFGANG VON GOETHE

For a seed to grow and thrive, it is imperative that you provide it with fertile soil and the optimal conditions for growth. In the case of planting the seeds of kindness in business, this means starting with a strong foundation built on people-first principles, core values and integral leadership capable of withstanding mergers, downsizing, role repositioning, business realignment strategies and the worst-case scenario, staff layoffs. The more people you involve in championing this vision, the stronger your foundation will be and the greater your likelihood of success.

# Ideas for planting the seeds of kindness in business

- Create a "kindness corner" bulletin board in the staff room or lounge area. Invite staff members to contribute inspiring thoughts, quotes, suggestions, positive newsworthy events and articles. Attract attention to the kindness corner by decorating it with vibrant colours, imagery and symbols along the theme of kindness.

- Start a "random acts of kindness" campaign in conjunction with the annual World Kindness Day held on November 13. Involve staff members, customers and friends. This day was declared by the World Kindness Movement to serve as a springboard and focus for kindness activities. The beauty of this day is that it was established to acknowledge the fundamental importance of kindness in a satisfying and meaningful life. Another purpose was to join together individuals and nations across the globe in creating a more compassionate world.

- Host "Lunch and Learn" presentations. This is a great way to foster friendships and more caring connections between colleagues through the exploration of personal development themes. Suggested themes include:

  1. Nutrition: Wholesome Meals for Busy Folks, Heart-Smart Cooking
  2. Themes on physical, mental, emotional and spiritual health
  3. Stress management
  4. Seasonal themes: gardening tips, Christmas hosting and decorating ideas
  5. Parenting issues
  6. Journal writing

If you have multiple units decentralized from your head office location, arrange mail-outs to post on their bulletin boards, or invite speakers in during staff meetings when everyone is together. Make use of their local communities.

# STAGE TWO: cultivating kindness in business

*To cultivate kindness
is a valuable part of the business of life.*

—SAMUEL JOHNSON

Once the seeds have been planted, you need to tend to their growth in order to ensure the success of your garden. Cultivating kindness in business involves fostering the growth of a caring workplace, one in which colleagues not only see each other for what they do, but also for who they are. Creating friendships at work is the action of creating kindness in business. We need to explore ways to hold each other responsible and accountable for nurturing positive, friendly working relationships.

Seek out goodwill ambassadors to assist and support you in the journey to a kinder workplace. Look around and grow friendships. Find ways to recognize, honor and celebrate the uniqueness of the individuals that make up your workplace. In human nature, as in nature, it is this diversity that strengthens and enriches our environment and enables us not only to survive, but also to thrive.

## Ideas for cultivating kindness in business

♦ Create a workplace Kindness to Colleagues intranet site where everything from wellness ideas to kindness tips and stories can be shared and accessed. Solicit the support of your in-house technology staff in developing the site, and solicit ideas from the frontline staff to executives on how to make it appealing and magical. You will discover that as your colleagues begin to tap into this site, they will soon find themselves looking forward to the "good news" site at work.

♦ Start a "Wellness and Personal Growth" library at your location. Talk to key players in training and development, human resources and staff social committees about covering the costs for the library setup. If funding is not available, ask people to donate used books in the categories you need. You will be surprised by how many people are willing to share the books that brought them joy, self-discovery and learning.

♦ Seek to link or integrate your kindness program with other existing in-house programs such as employee or community-centered rewards, recognition programs and events. Work toward getting buy-in from the leadership teams in marketing and sales, public relations, accounting, operations, human resources and other departments.

♦ Host "Lunch and Learn" presentations with advanced themes in personal development. Suggested themes include:

1.  Family dynamics
2.  Cultivating gratitude
3.  Career resilience
4.  Ethics in the workplace
5.  Upward, downward and lateral communication skills
6.  Yoga and relaxation techniques
7.  Creativity and innovation
8.  The importance of apologies

♦ Start a "Kindness in Business" diary. Circulate it around your department or location, collecting thoughts and stories. Hold a mini celebration and share the contents with everyone when the diary is complete.

# STAGE THREE: harvesting kindness in business

*Constant kindness can accomplish much.*
*As the sun makes ice melt,*
*kindness causes misunderstanding,*
*mistrust and hostility to evaporate.*

—ALBERT SCHWEITZER

To produce a successful harvest, it takes the committed contribution and skills of many people. It also requires an understanding of one's environment and a willingness to adapt to change by exploring new ways of doing things. In the farming environment, the "higher ground farmer" ensures the continued health and fertility of the land for future generations by rotating the crops and working with new varieties of plants that support the others' seasonal growth.

Likewise, if you want to bring your workplace to a higher ground and ensure its continued health and productivity, you need to be willing to work with your workforce's changing needs and nurture their sense of community. Harvest season is a time for gathering the product of your labor, bringing the community together and celebrating your successes.

## Ideas for harvesting kindness in business

- ♦ Organize a week-long Kindness to Colleagues campaign by encouraging everyone to commit random acts of kindness in the three themed areas: kindness to oneself, colleagues and in the community. Link the campaign to raising awareness about World Kindness Day on November 13.

- ♦ Integrate an antiviolence program with existing Occupational Health and Safety initiatives. Research antiviolence and awareness training programs that will support your organization.

- ♦ Start a social committee and plan fun adventures and activities to bring people together.

- Start a wellness program in-house by forming a committee of excited volunteers and put your thinking caps on. Start researching program success stories locally and globally to draw ideas from.

- Champion a community-oriented program that hasn't been done in your organization before by starting a "volunteers needed" drive. Do something bold and big like building a house for Habitat for Humanity.

- Host "Lunch and Learn" presentations with advanced themes in personal development. Suggested themes include:

1. Forgiveness in the workplace
2. Living life fully
3. Financial planning
4. Discovering your values at work
5. Creating purpose-filled workplaces
6. Authenticity in the workplace
7. Self-esteem and self-confidence

## How to get your organization on board

The more sensitive you are to management's organizational objectives and challenges, the greater your likelihood of obtaining the support you need to drive your initiative to successful fruition. Before trying to launch a kindness initiative, you need to first get to know the players. Begin by talking to your immediate supervisors and soliciting their feedback. You might be surprised at what great suggestions you get before you move on to the next step.

## Create your network of support

♦ Test out your program idea with a few colleagues. Solicit their feedback and ideas. This will not only give you the courage to proceed to senior management, but will also provide you with a chance to practice your presentation in a safe and open environment.

♦ Once you have tested the water, the next step is to know who your supporters are on the management team and approach them.

♦ Be sensitive to your organization's specific culture. When driving an initiative, put yourself in the shoes of management and see the project idea from their perspective. For example, ask yourself how a kindness initiative could benefit areas within your organization, such as marketing, sales, public relations, communications and human resources.

## Use a top-down timed approach for buy-in

Senior management buy-in is imperative for a new concept or idea to fly. Once you have refined your presentation, your timing in presenting the concept will be key. In some business environments, the end, the middle and the first of the month are not optimal times for capturing interest, as leaders may be preoccupied with financial budgets and monthly wrap-ups. Their receptiveness to your idea may also be influenced by how other matters fared that month. Timing is everything. It is worth waiting for the right time to present your idea, for example, when you see a gap or need and can present a compelling case to fill this void. The higher you climb, the harder the wind blows, so the first rules of launching a successful kindness campaign are patience, understanding and great timing.

## Be prepared to champion your idea

Any new idea needs a champion to get it started and to keep the momentum going. Once you initiate the process, you need to be prepared to personally drive it, or else find someone within your organization who believes in your vision strongly enough to co-champion it with you.

It takes courage, time, persistence and patience to move your initiative forward. View this as an amazing personal growth time for yourself and a chance to be in a position to influence change. If you want to taste the best fruit, sometimes you have to go out on a limb to get it. Action is courage actualized!

## Gather your kindness committee team

Gathering the right committee to move your initiative forward is integral to your program's success. Ask yourself if team members are "like-minded"; do they share your values, mission and the vision of the organizations? To attract these individuals to your cause, be clear with yourself on your own values and vision. Consider having the team come up with a couple of core values. Such clarification is important to ensure all team members agree. This makes it easier to determine which actions and decisions are in line with the values, and which are not.

In choosing your team, you may wish to consider the following questions:

- ◆ Do you have specific individuals in mind to round out the team?
- ◆ Do you have players with complementary strengths?
- ◆ What kind of personalities are you looking for?
- ◆ Are these individuals aligned with the vision, values and purpose of this initiative?
- ◆ What level of understanding do you have of how to work with people in a volunteer capacity?
- ◆ What can you learn to make this easier for you and them?
- ◆ Do you have a good gender and diversity balance on the team?

## How to develop an inspirational vision

Developing an inspirational vision is critical to igniting the energy and commitment necessary to drive an initiative and ensure its long-term sustainability. To inspire, a vision must be vivid and heartfelt, and must rest on a strong foundation of core values. It must focus not on the benefits for the individual or a small group, but on the contribution and legacy that will be left behind for others to enjoy for years to come.

Answer the following questions to help build an inspirational vision. Better yet, answer them with your team and build a vision together that will bring out the best everyone has to offer:

1. Where do you see this project in one year? In three years?
2. How will it impact your organization?
3. How will it impact your team of volunteers? Your department?
4. How will it impact you personally?
5. Is this vision one that will inspire you to keep going despite rejection, ridicule, setbacks, delays and all other hardships?

*Write a short vision statement that succinctly describes what this kindness initiative will look like in your organization when it is fully operational.*

_____

_____

_____

_____

_____

_____

_____

_____

# TEN WAYS TO INSPIRE COMMITMENT IN YOUR VOLUNTEERS

1. *Start with shared values.*

   * Share your vision and then build on it together. It belongs to everyone. Get them excited to be on your team.

2. *Care about them personally, not just professionally.*

   * Volunteer work helps us grow personally as well as improving our work-related competencies. Remember, volunteers don't always want everything to be about work.
   * Take off your business hat. Be authentic and show them you care. Your example will inspire them to care about others on the team.

3. *Help them discover their passion for why they are on a kindness initiative.*

   * Ask them what they want and need from this experience. Be prepared to look for ways to help them achieve this.
   * Make sure they are working toward their own goals. This will keep them further engaged.

4. *Encourage everyone to share their natural gifts and talents.*

   * Ask them to write down their gifts and talents and share them with the group at the beginning of the project.
   * Ask them to pick the project pieces that accentuate their gifts and talents, or an area in which they would like to grow.

5. *Always be present.*

   * Listen, listen some more and listen again.
   * Put aside your own agenda and forget about having to "accomplish" something over being present with the person in front of you.

6.  *Don't squelch ideas and suggestions.*

    *   There are no dumb questions or ideas. Establish these guidelines in the beginning.
    *   Respect and listen carefully to all suggestions and ideas. Implement bits and pieces of them if you can't incorporate them all. This will keep everyone enthusiastic, participating and bringing forward their suggestions.

7.  *Allow for creative license during your meetings.*

    *   Put toys, doodle pads and crayons out on the table. Find ways to stimulate creative thinking.
    *   Facilitate creative thinking and experiential exercises at each meeting. Take turns facilitating this process.

8.  *Recognize and reward.*

    *   Find ways to reward your team with small incentives and gifts. It is the thought that counts, not the price of the gift. A box of chocolates can do wonders.
    *   Recognize each person's individual contribution for their portion of the initiative. Spend time celebrating successes on team efforts as well.

9.  *Be prepared.*

    *   Be organized with your material for each meeting. Share this responsibility if appropriate so everyone participates equally and learns.
    *   Keep the meeting flowing naturally so that time isn't wasted. Become effective, effervescent and, of course, efficient — don't waste valuable time.

10. *Make your meetings fun to attend.*

    *   Laughter is the best motivator. Personalize your meetings. Balance having fun with getting things done.

## Use a bottom-up approach for implementation

While it is important to get senior management buy-in in order to proceed with your program, be prepared to physically implement the program without their presence. The reality is that your senior management members are involved in a number of other initiatives and may not attend your events or visibly show ongoing support for your program. Know this doesn't mean they don't care; it just means they are busy and in some cases they haven't bought into the concept yet and that is okay. Over time, as your program matures and produces results, you will find that this situation changes.

History has shown that marvelous ideas and change occur from a grassroots approach. This simply means "from the ground up." Remember the simple rule that strength comes in numbers and there are far more people at the front line in an organization than in management. This is the level at which the ideas and concepts are put into action, once the approval and support have been obtained, initiate a frontline movement with the aim of raising awareness for a kinder workplace.

Be prepared to work on a shoestring budget at first, because kindness shouldn't cost anything. The idea is to build momentum progressively for your program, year to year. Don't get discouraged if you discern that there is little, if any, funding available for you and your committee. It's easy to invent an idea, but it takes special innovation and creativity to make it work. Management will be impressed when they see you are committed enough to the program to move it forward on a shoestring budget. Take inventory of all of your resources. Funding from your organization is just one form of support. Consider the alternatives:

- Do you have an internal department that could develop materials such as posters, banners and documents? What about an in-house intranet site and technology department support?

- Are there companies or suppliers that might benefit from sponsoring or supporting this initiative?

- Do you have access to free or "at cost" merchandise to use as giveaways and incentives? Can you barter?

♦ Can you bring in professionals to share their knowledge at "Lunch and Learn" presentations in exchange for the free promotion of their service?

♦ Remember, the list is endless and so are the possibilities.

Kindness starts with a state of mind, on which you can't put a price tag. Don't limit yourself by believing that only a well-funded program will have impact. That has stopped many projects and creative ideas from growing from a spark into a fire. Never underestimate the committee's ability to reach people.

## Work within the organizational culture

When launching an initiative, work within the limits of the corporate culture. Culture describes how an organization does business internally. Honor protocol and etiquette if you want a new initiative to be accepted. This doesn't mean there isn't room to expand and change the culture, only that sensitivity is important to drive your campaign effectively.

The Kindness to Colleagues campaign is meant to enhance, support and strengthen the culture. By being aware and sensitive to the culture, you increase your chances of successfully integrating the program into the organizational fiber. It is also important to become an example of kindness in business by seeking to understand your surroundings and by honoring where people are coming from.

## Ask yourself:

***What does our organizational culture look like, feel like, sound like?***

_____

_____

_____

_____

***How does this program enhance our culture and where can all or some of it fit in?***

_____

_____

_____

_____

***Who can I consult who really understands our culture?***

_____

_____

_____

## Link to other organizational initiatives

You are only as strong as the weakest link in the chain. Any program that stands in a silo will likely die in a silo. Linking the Kindness to Colleagues program with existing initiatives in your organization will secure its survival through the ups and downs of your organization and make it easier for you to "sell" the idea to senior management. Finding ways to weave the program into other corporate initiatives is the key to ensuring its long-term sustainability.

Look for natural links such as the following:

- **Occupational Health and Safety.** If you are legislated under the Violence in the Workplace Act, then it is a natural fit to link it as an antiviolence program.

- **Corporate wellness programs.** The program will work as a Kindness to Oneself initiative.

- **In-house reward and recognition programs.** Can you link the program with sales and marketing reward programs, or recruitment and retention programs?

## Survey first, then proceed

First, send out a letter to survey the climate for acceptance, and to ask key participants what they think of the initiative. Introduce the topic; make your letter compelling and interesting to grab their attention and their desire to participate. Key participants include managers and supervisors; you will need their support to get the individual business units or departments to participate. You don't need 100 percent support to proceed. Even 20 percent participation has an impact.

Customize the following letter, then send it to department leaders or locations to introduce the idea of launching a Kindness to Colleagues initiative within your workplace. Solicit feedback before proceeding, to help you gauge the "climate" and receptiveness to the concept. By taking a "heads-up" approach to a kindness initiative, you will gain more support for driving the program forward.

SAMPLE LETTER INTRODUCING A

# KINDNESS TO COLLEAGUES INITIATIVE

(Insert your personal introduction first.)

California journalist Anne Herbert sparked the Kindness Movement in North America in the early 1980s. She coined the phrase, "Practice random kindness and senseless acts of beauty." Anne Herbert grew tired of continual news of random acts of violence on the news, and decided to counter this negativity by promoting random acts of kindness. Convinced that people needed to hear more good news, she started to write about kindness, and encouraged her readers to join in the action. Stories of random acts of kindness started to flood in from around the continent. Examples included allowing someone into a lineup, anonymously paying for someone's coffee in a coffee shop, and putting money in a stranger's expired parking meter to spare them a fine.

In 1993, Conari Press published a book entitled *Random Acts of Kindness*. On the back of the book was inscribed, "Join the Kindness Revolution." Within six months, Conari received tens of thousands of letters from people saying they wanted to join the Kindness Revolution. The Kindness Movement has since grown to include over 600 communities in the U.S.A. and Canada.

The Kindness Movement also has its roots in other countries. In 1997, The World Kindness Movement was formed at an international kindness conference hosted by the over thirty-year-old Small Kindness Movement in Japan. Founding countries included Canada, U.S.A., Australia, Singapore, Japan, South Korea, England and Thailand. The World Kindness Movement was established to acknowledge the fundamental importance of kindness for a satisfying and meaningful life. In order to provide a focus and springboard for the promotion of kindness, November 13 was declared World Kindness Day.

How can our organization can get involved in creating a kinder, more harmonious and fulfilling workplace?

Our organization has some amazing people-driven initiatives that spur us to create more respect, more awareness and greater synergy with our in-house programs, so as to strengthen their effectiveness and impact.

The Kindness to Colleagues workplace initiative links our programs under one actionable umbrella — kindness. The program focuses on three key areas:

- **Kindness to Colleagues**, which links in-house programs such as sexual harassment, diversity and respectful workplace initiatives. (Insert your company's current programs in this area.)

- **Kindness in our Community** locally and globally, which links in-house community and worldwide awareness programs and sponsorship initiatives (Insert your organization's community initiatives.)

- **Kindness to Oneself**, which links in-house wellness programs and Occupational Health and Safety initiatives. (Insert your organization's community initiatives.)

The Kindness to Colleagues initiative will also provide departments and organizations with concrete ways to actively support and translate these program ideas and concepts into action.

*(Insert your proposed plan of action. Are you planning to hold a one-day kindness campaign in conjunction with World Kindness Day or a weeklong celebration? Over what period of time will you build momentum? Will you be tying the campaign in with an existing rewards and recognition program or special event?)*

Thank you. We value your input and would like your feedback on whether you believe this is worthwhile and are willing to support us in proceeding with our initiative. We welcome any comments you have on how we can make this initiative a success.

Sincerely,

Your Name
Organization

## Create a user-friendly process

In today's workplace, there is always so much coming down the pipeline requiring immediate attention that it is fully understandable management could initially perceive a new initiative as yet another thing that requires "doing," or the "flavor of the month." Creating a user-friendly process, with the end user in mind, will increase your likelihood of gaining support and inspiring participation.

Here are a few tips for creating a user-friendly process.

- Find out how information is most effectively delivered in your organization.
- Be prepared with both hard-copy kits and electronic files of your campaign, as individuals vary in how they learn and take in information.
- Lay out all the information in an easy-to-follow, step-by-step process, so that anyone can pick it up and get started. Use the K.I.S.S. method (Keep It Short and Simple).
- Find leaders who will act as a champion and serve as a source of inspiration and information. Create a list of these champions and stay in touch.

# NOMINATION FORM

This sample form can get you started on holding a Kindness to Colleagues day, week or month. Encourage colleagues to submit stories of colleagues committing kind acts.

Nominate your colleague or yourself in one or more of the three kindness themes:

1. **Kindness to Oneself:** Look for colleagues who are actively involved in self-care, well-being and the nurturing of their inner spirit.

2. **Kindness to Colleagues:** Look for colleagues treating each other with mutual care and respect.

3. **Kindness in the Community, locally and globally:** Look for colleagues actively involved in making a difference through community service.

## Procedure:

♦ Write your kind-act story and fill in the form details.

♦ Submit the completed form by email to (insert address here) or send it to (insert your department or the name of the individual who will collect these).

| NOMINATOR NAME & DEPT | NOMINEE NAME & DEPT | CATEGORY NOMINATED IN |
|---|---|---|
| | | ♦ **Kindness to Oneself**<br>♦ **Kindness to Colleagues**<br>♦ **Kindness in the Community** |

**Share Your Story**

## Gather measurable results

Tracking the results is imperative for long-term success and could be a determining factor in management's decision to run the initiative in the future. Certain program successes may be harder to quantify than others. Keep in mind that it takes effort from a number of arenas and initiatives to see tangible results in such areas as disability claims, workers' compensation claims, grievances, employee turnover and employee opinion surveys. Gather all the evidence possible to help support your position that this initiative is making a significant difference. You may choose to:

♦ Hold a contest that encourages individuals within the organization to commit acts of kindness. As you collect the stories of kindness, share them over the intranet to create further enthusiasm and recognition for the program. Keep a record of the stories, and highlight profound ones.

♦ Survey individuals within different departments or branches for feedback on how the kindness initiative has impacted them. This will help you document what worked, and help refine the program for the future.

♦ Create a pre and post survey and compare the difference.

## Compassion, connection and community

Ultimately, this is the thread that binds all of these pages together; compassion, connection and community. These three gentle, provocative, yet profoundly powerful words have an ability to transform the world of work as we know it today.

This book was written for the leader in all of us, regardless of what our job description reads. As John Quincy Adams reminds us, "if your actions inspire others to dream more, learn more, do more and become more, you are a leader." We need more champions with the will and courage to change the workplace, one kind act at a time.

In parting, I leave you with a question: when was the last time you committed a random act of kindness for yourself, your colleagues or your community?

I warmly challenge you to put this book down, and in the next 48 hours, stand up for an ideal and send forth a tiny ripple of hope.

We live, we learn, we laugh.

Olivia

*"Live your life so that your children*
*can tell their children that you not*
*only stood for something wonderful-*
*you acted on it"*

———Dan Zadra

# Appendix
# Kindness Quotes

*"No act of kindness, no matter how small, is ever wasted."*

——AESOP

*"Kindness is a language which the deaf can hear and the blind can read."*

——MARK TWAIN

*"The flower of kindness will grow. Maybe not now, but it will some day. And in that kindness will flow, for kindness grows in this way."*

——ROBERTA ALAN

*"A kind and compassionate act is often its own rewards."*

——WILLIAM JOHN BENNET

*"Have you had a kindness shown? Pass it on; 'twas not given for thee alone, pass it on. Let it travel down the years, let it wipe another's tears, till in heaven the deed appears, pass it on."*

–Henry Burton

*"Fair and softly goes far."*

—Miguel de Cervantes

*"If you were busy being kind, before you knew it, you would find you'd soon forget to think 'twas true that someone was unkind to you. If you were busy being glad, and cheering people who are sad, although your heart might ache a bit, you'd soon forget to notice it."*

—R. Foreman

*"As perfume to the flower, so is kindness to speech."*

—Katherine Francke

*"Kindness is the golden chain by which society is bound together."*

—Johan Wolfgang Von Goethe

*"A kind heart is a fountain of gladness, making everything in its vicinity into smiles."*

—Washington Irving

*"Let no one ever come to you without leaving better and happier. Be the living expression of kindness: kindness in your face, kindness in your eyes, kindness in your smile."*

—MOTHER TERESA

*"If you have not often felt the joy of doing a kind act, you have neglected much, and most of all yourself."*

—A. NEILEN

*"Kind words do not cost much. Yet they accomplish much."*

—BLAIRE PASCAL

*"One can pay back the loan of gold, but one lies forever in debt to those who are kind."*

—MALAYAN PROVERB

*"Kindness has more power than compulsion."*

—ANONYMOUS

*"If your words are soft and sweet, they won't be as hard to swallow if you have to eat them."*

—ANONYMOUS

*"Kindness is tenderness. Kindness is love, but perhaps greater than love. Kindness is good will."*

——RANDOLPH RAY

*"Kindness consists in loving people more than they deserve."*

—JACQUELINE SCHIFF

*"One who knows how to show and to accept kindness will be a friend better than any possession."*

——SOPHOCLES

*"Kindness is an inner desire that makes us want to do good things even if we do not get anything in return. It is the joy of our life to do them. When we do good things from this inner desire, there is kindness in everything we think, say, want and do."*

—EMANUEL SWEDENBORG

*"You can accomplish by kindness what you cannot by force."*

——PUBLILIUS SYRUS

"*Be gentle to all, and stern with yourself.*"

—ST. TERESA OF AVILA

"*Business will continue to go where invited and remain were appreciated.*"

—ANONYMOUS

"*Kindness and honesty can only be expected from the strong.*"

—ANONYMOUS

"*Do all the good you can. By all the means you can. In all the ways you can. In all the places you can. At all the times you can. To all the people you can. As long as ever you can.*"

—JOHN WESLEY

"*Little kindnesses. . . will broaden your heart, and slowly you will habituate yourself to helping your fellow man in many ways.*"

—ANONYMOUS

"*Weakness of attitude becomes weakness of character*"

—ALBERT EINSTEIN

# Recommended Reading

## KINDNESS TO ONESELF

**Downshifting:** *How to Work Less and Save More*, John D. Drake

**Eight Weeks to Optimum Health,** Andrew Weil

**Food and the Emotional Connection**, Kristina Sisu

**Keeping Life Simple**: *7 Guiding Principles and 500 Tips and Ideas,* Karen Levine

**Massage for Busy People,** Dawn Groves

**Mastery of Stress:** *Relaxation in the Workplace*, Paul Skye

**Reality Fitness**, Nicki Anderson

**Say Goodnight to Insomnia:** *The Six Week Solution*, Gregg D. Jacobs

**Second Innocence**: Rediscovering Joy and Wonder, John B. Izzo, Ph.D.

**Seeking Your Healthy Balance**, Donald Tubesing

**Short Cuts to Success,** Jonathan Robinson

**Simplify Your Work Life,** Elaine St. James

**Simple Living in a Complex World**, David Irvine

*The Art of Doing Nothing*, Veronique Vienne

*The Truth about Burnout*, Christina Masiach

*22 Keys to Creating a Meaningful Workplace*, Tom Terez

*Working from the Heart*, Jacqueline McMakin

# KINDNESS TO COLLEAGUES

*Awakening Corporate Soul*, John Izzo

*Chicken Soup for the Soul at Work*, Jack Canfield

*Colorful Personalities*, George J. Boelcke

*Community of Kindness*, Conari Press

*Common Kindness*, Janet Hopkins

*Learning How to Be Kind to Others*, Susan Kent

*Practice of Kindness*, Conari Press

*Random Acts of Kindness*, Conari Press

*Soul of Kindness*, Marc Barasch

*Sowing in Silence: 101 Ways to Sow Seeds of Kindness*, Cheryl Hicks

*Stone Soup for the World*, Marianne Lerned

*The Art of Happiness at Work*, Dalai Lama

*The Heart Aroused*, David Whyte

*The Hidden Power of Kindness*, Lawrence G. Lavasik

*The Stirring of Soul in the Workplace*, Alan Briskin

*The Soul of Business*, Michael Toms and Justine Willis Toms

*Turning to One Another*, Margaret Wheatley

# KINDNESS IN THE COMMUNITY

*Acts of Balance,* Grant Copeland

*Circles of Strength,* Helen Forsey

*Cool to Be Kind,* The Kindness Crew

*Conscious Evolution,* Barbara Marx

*Earth Future,* Guy Douncey

*Greenpeace,* Rex Weyler

*Heart at Work,* Jack Canfield

*Inspirational Leadership,* Lance Secretan

*Investing in the Common Good,* Susan Meeker-Lawry

*Leadership in a Challenging World,* Barbara Shipka

*Love and Profit: The Art of Caring Leadership,* James A. Autry

*Managing by Values,* Ken Blanchard

*One World, One Earth,* Merryl Hammond

*Street Reclaiming,* David Engwicht

*The Lexus and the Olive Tree,* Thomas C. Friedman

*The Natural Step,* Brian Nattrass

*Values Shift: The New Work Ethic and What It Means for Business,*
   John B. Izzo, Ph.D. and Pam Withers.

# Additional Book References

The following titles have been provided should you wish to delve further into the topic of creating engaged workplaces by addressing violence in the workplace.

***Brutal Bosses,*** Harvey A. Hornstein

***The Bully at Work,*** Andrea Adams

***Bully in Sight,*** Tim Field

***Human Resources Guide to Preventing Workplace Violence,*** Norman A. Keith

***Mobbing in the Workplace,*** Noa Davenport

***Toxic Emotions at Work,*** Peter J. Frost

***Work Rage,*** Gerry Smith

# Internet Resources

## WORLD KINDNESS MOVEMENT WEBSITES

Australia: www.kindness.com.au

Canada: www.kindacts.net

India: www.kindnessunlimited.tripod.com

Nigeria: www.peace.ca/africa

Scotland: www.kindnesscotland.co.uk

Singapore: www.singaporekindness.org.sg

Thailand: www.Thaikindness.com

United Arab Emirates: www.hearts.ae

United States: www.actsofkindness.org

World Kindness Movement: www.worldkindness.org.sg

# Products and Services

## Great reward and recoginition ideas

Finding ways to motivate and inspire those around you can be as easy as simple gifts and services to support your kindness campaign.

**An Open Heart:** www.anopenheart.org

One of the most inspiring online stores you will come across. These products were created with the intention of spreading kindness and happiness professionally and personally. From Post-it notes to cards and T-shirts, these gifts are perfect as inspirational gifts to launch your initiative and keep it going.

**Baudville:** www.baudville.com

This online store's tagline is "Putting Applause on Paper," and it sells a great collection of corporate inspirational gifts suitable for all events, to show your gratitude in a large or small way.

**Compendium:** www.compendium.com

Higher-end products creating motivational workplaces: Look specifically for the Practice Kindness Cards: 30 Cards for 30 Days.

**EPraise:** www.epraiseexpress.com

A simple and easy high-tech way to build momentum for expressing gratitude and appreciation in your workplace. This online Web-based recognition system, for a minimal price, offers an ability to send email praise to colleagues, suppliers, customers. Select from over 100 colorful e-note designs.

**Healing Baskets:** www.healingbaskets.com

Great products for life and work, so make sure you check out their products in a section called *Job Loss*. This section consists of little thoughtful gifts for when a colleague loses their job, to cheer them up.

**Kindness Diaries:** www.kindnessinc@myway.com

These wonderful diaries are the combined work and inspiration of Mari-Lyn Hudson and Signature Printing of Edmonton, Alberta. They are an immediate way to start spreading kindness in the workplace.

**Mind My Body:** www.mindmybody.com

Here is an inexpensive and innovative way to encourage employees to stay fit and deal with obesity and diabetes, among other obesity-related health conditions. This program crosses both borders and provides inexpensive online and on-site coaching for health.

**Playfair:** www.playfair.com

A great site for ideas on making work more fun! Check out their "standing ovation" and commit to sending out some to your colleagues.

# Programs to support your kindness campaign

**Alliance of Work/Life Professionals:** www.awlp.org

A United States-based organization that strives to address rising life/work issues through publications, forums and professional development strategies by working to influence better integration of work and family life issues.

**Be Kind To Humankind:** www.bekindweek.org

What a gem of a website. If you need to be inspired to get started this website will support you all the way. Check out the 7 days of suggestions on how to practice kindness and get busy and participate in Be Kind to Humankind weekAugust 25-31.

**Extreme Kindness Crew:** www.extremekindness.com or www.kindnesscrew.com

Here are four young men making a difference one kind act a time and teaching others by their actions to do the same. They are looking for kindness champions to join their movement by taking up their challenge of starting a Kindness Crew in your own community or business. You can download their *Kindness Crew Kit* and start taking positive steps to creating change around you.

**Forgive for Good:** www.alllearn.org or www.learntoforgive.com

Take the online, exceptional, five-week program on learning how to forgive and let go.

**Global Classroom Connection:** www.classroom-connection.org

Here is a beautiful initiative to connect school age children around the world via the internet. Their powerful mandate is to create a global classroom to help bring cross cultural experiences to children and to develop lasting friendships between students around the world. Their tag line says it all: bringing the youth of the world together, one classroom at a time.

**Kinder World Coin-spiracy:** www.investinakinderworld.com

The Invest in a Kinder World Coin-spiracy is a program developed for schools and youth groups to raise awareness on how kind acts can create positive global change. Purchase a coin for your school and start committing random acts of kindness around the globe.

**Museum of Tolerance:** www.museumoftolerance.com

Not only is this an experiential, interactive museum working to eliminate racism and hatred, but it also offers programs for educators, law enforcement and the corporate sectors. Check out *Tools for Tolerance,* which provides transformational workplace learning and leadership development to challenge individuals in redefining their roles in a changing world.

**Non-violent Communication:** www.nonviolentcommunication.com

A global organization whose vision is to support a world where individuals are getting their needs met and resolving their conflicts peacefully through innovative and life-altering techniques in conflict resolution, starting with compassion.

**One Human Family:** www.onehumanfamily.info

Making a difference, one bumper sticker at a time. This nonprofit all-volunteer organization has already sent out over 600,000 free bumper stickers that boldly state "All People are Created Equal Members of One Human Family. Order them for free and if you can support their vision, by sending along a donation. If you can't, don't worry about it, they will forward you the stickers regardless. There is one key expectation that goes with the stickers, you must give them away free of charge and can't profit through the distribution of the stickers.

**Pay It Forward:** www.payitforward.org

Check out this amazing array of kindness stories of individuals like you and me who have chosen to pay a kindness forwards. Its so inspiring you won't be able to stop reading them.

**S.T.O.P. the Violence and Bullying:** www.thestopproject.com

Riley Inge has been touring schools and workplaces with his successful Steps To Overcoming Problems (STOP) program, discussing self-esteem, coping skills and conflict resolution. STOP has developed a unique approach through music with thought-provoking rap lyrics and visual messages to reach kids between the ages of four and nineteen.

**The Apologist:** www.The-Apologist.co.uk

Try using this site to practice apologizing. Eventually you might feel comfortable talking to the potential recipient in person and speaking your truth.

**The Canadian Health Network:** www.canadian-health-network.ca

A Canadian government-sponsored website whose mission is to support Canadians in making informed choices about their health, by providing access to multiple sources of credible and practical e-health information.

**The National Quality Institute of Canada:** www.nqi.ca

A premier Canadian information site that provides organizations with strategic business frameworks, services and tools to support improvements in quality and healthy workplace environments.

**The Wellness Counsel of America:** www.welcoa.org

A United States premier resource supporting workplace wellness initiatives with a dedication to helping organizations of all sizes build and sustain wellness programs.

**Virtues Project:** www.virtuesproject.com

A powerful international initiative that strives to empower individuals to learn and live by their core values. Inspired by three individuals wanting to do something about the rising violence in and around families.

# Share your "Kindness in Business" story or initiative

Help us spread the good news about kindness in business by sharing your story of how a kind act had a positive impact on you, your colleagues or your community. Also, we would love to hear of any organizational wellness or kindness campaigns your business has initiated.

If the story you submit is selected, it may be published on our website or in newsletters, or newspapers, or shared during speaking engagements. If you wish your name to remain confidential, or have any other concerns, please indicate them at the very beginning of your story, and include your full contact information so that we can contact you if necessary.

To submit your story, simply write to us at www.inspirationalhr.com.

# About the Author

Olivia McIvor's successful 23-year career in business management has been supported by a 19 year background in the field of Human Resource Management and Leadership.

Her approach to people management is as innovative as it is creative. Combine that with her philosophical mind and her vast library of experiences and you have a unique blend inspiring management. Her diverse background includes progressive careers in retail and tourism prior to establishing a name in the financial industry as the 'human touch' HR Director. It was here that she pioneered and spearheaded the implementation of numerous innovative workplace wellness and employee engagement initiatives within the financial sector with outstanding results. Ms. McIvor has gained valuable experience working in union/non-unionized environments and working with a wide range of diversity in many sectors.

In 2000 Olivia ventured into the Entrepreneur world herself as the owner of a unique bookstore devoted to Personal and Professional Leadership. In 2001 Olivia was nominated *Female Entrepreneur of the Year* by **Working Women Magazine** and has been featured on the Knowledge Network/Discovery Channel for a segment on workplace wellness. Her speaking endeavors have included numerous conferences including the *US Food Service, The Georgia Power Company, Family Services of Ontario, Credit Union Central of BC and Saskatchewan, Capital Savings & Credit Union, Health Work and Wellness Conference, UBC Symposium on Wellness, Soul @ Work, The Good Samaritan Society and many others.* She has trained, consulted and spoken to numerous associations, organizations and conferences across North America.

She is president of McIvor & Company consulting and is a senior consultant, facilitator and presenter with The Izzo Group Ltd. were over the past five years has engaged audiences with her inspiring and thought provoking programs on *"Four Generations, One Workplace"*, *"Branding from the Inside Out"* , *" Leadership: It's All About Building Character"*, *Kindness: Creating Safe, Healthy and Vibrant Workplaces"* and *"People Centered Leadership: Management for Engagement"* and *"Renewing the Spirit at Work Program"*.

Ms. McIvor lives in Vancouver, British Columbia.

# Working with Ms. McIvor

At McIvor & Company our philosophy is simple, we believe in the power of people. In our work with clients, we make a positive impact on the business world every day. We believe great results start with great leadership and its only through building strong foundations from the frontline to the bottom line that results are achieved. Our team is committed to helping companies increase their productivity through creating engaged and inspired employees.

- **Our Vision:** To support workplaces in creating safe, healthy and vibrant environments where people can thrive and achieve their full potential.
- **Our Intention:** To create a passion wave for the continued humanization of the workplace. We do this by diligently striving to put the 'human' back into Human Resources.

For more information on Ms. McIvor presenting at your conference or working with your company, please visit: ***www.inspirationalhr.com***

# Ordering copies of this book

_Trade Retailers:_

Please call:
**FairWinds Press & Distributors**
**1-604-913-0649**
*www.fairwinds-press.com*
*info@fairwinds-press.com*


*www.fairwinds-press.com*
**PO Box 668 Lions Bay, BC. V0N2E0**
**Canada**

FAIRWINDS PRESS

The Business of Kindness

# Bibliography

Adams, Scott. *The Dilbert Principle: Cubicle's-Eye View of Bosses, Meetings, Management Fads, and Other Workplace Afflictions*. New York: Harper & Brothers, 1996.

Blanchard, Kenneth. *The One Minute Manager*. New York: William Morrow & Co,1981.

Buckingham, Marcus and Curt Coffman. *First Break All the Rules*. Markham, Ont.: Simon & Schuster, 1999.

Buscaglia, Leo. *Love*. New York: Fawcett Crest, 1972.

Carol, Lewis. *Alice In Wonderland*. New York: Lewis Carroll and Martin Gardner Signet Classics, Re-issue edition 2000.

Collier, Lindsay. *Get Our of Your Thinking Box: 365 Ways to Brighten Your Life and Enhance Your Creativity*. San Franscico, Ca: Robert D. Reed Publishers, 1994.

Cooperrider, Dr. David and Diana Whitney. *Appreciative Inquiry*. San Francisco: Berrett Koehler Publishers, 2005.

Conari Press. *Random Acts of Kindness*. Berkley, CA: Conari Press, 1993.

Davenport, Noah, Ruth D. Schwart and Gail Pursell Elliott. *Emotional Abuse in the American Workplace*. Civil Society Publishing, 1999.

De Angelis, Barbara. *Confidence: Finding It and Living It*. Carlsbad, CA: Hay House, 1995.

de Saint-Exupéry, Antoine. *The Little Prince*. Harcourt Inc ,1943

Drouin, Dr. Hugh and David Rivard. *No Stone Unturned*. Family Services of Ontario,1997.

Field, Tim. *Bully In Sight How to Predict, Resist, Challenge and Combat Workplace Bullying*. Success Unlimited, 1996.

Fox, Mathew. *A Spirituality Named Compassion*. Rochester: Inner Traditions, 1999

Frankl, Victor E. *Man's Search for Meaning*. New York: Washington Square Press, 1959.

Fulghum, Robert. *All I Really Need To Know I Learned in Kindergarten: Uncommon Thoughts on Common Things.* New York: Random House, 2003.

Harvey A. Hornstein. *Brutal Bosses, and Their Prey.* New York: The Berkley Publishing Group, 1996.

Izzo, Dr. John B. & Pam Withers. *Values Shift, The New Work Ethic and What it Means for Business.* Vancouver, BC: FairWinds Press, 2000.

Keith. Norman A. *Human Resources Guide to Preventing Workplace Violence.* Aurora Professional Press, 1999.

Lama, Dalai and Victor Chan. *The Wisdom of Forgiveness: Intimate Journey's and Conversations.* New York: Penguin Group, 2004.

Lozoff, Bo. *It's a Meaningful Life.* Boston, MA.: Harvard Business School Press, 1997

Luskin, Dr. Fred. *Forgive For Good; A Proven Prescription for Health and Happiness.* New York: HarperCollins, 2003.

Patel, Mansukh. *Imagine...World Peace: A Peace Formula for All Nations.* Vancouver, BC: Raincoast Books, 2004.

Rayner, Jay *The Apologist. New Delhi:* Atlantic Books, 2005.

Reynolds, David K. *Constructive Living.* Hawaii, USA: University of Hawaii, 1984.

Rosenberg , Marshall B. *Non-Violent Communication.* Encinitas, CA: Puddledancer Press, 2003.

Schaar, John H. *Legitimacy on the Modern State.* Somerset, NJ: Transaction Publishers, Reprint edition, 1981.

Sisu, Kristina *Food and the Emotional Connection Using Your Relationship With Food as a Window Into the Psyche.* Santa Cruz, CA: Seraphine Publishing, 2002.

Smith, Gerry, Work Rage, *Identify the Problems, Implement the Solutions.* New York: Harper Collins, 2000.

Steinman, Gloria. *Revolution from Within: A Book of Self-Esteem.* Lancaster Place, London: Little, Brown and Company; Reprint edition, 1992.

Ulrich, David. *Human Resource Champions.* Boston, MA: Harvard Business School Press, 1997.

Weyler, Rex. *Greenpeace: How a Group of Journalists, Ecologists, and Visionaries Changed the World.* Vancouver, BC: Raincoast Books, 2004.

Wheatley, Margaret J. *Turning to One Another, Simple Conversations to Restore Hope to the Future.* San Francisco: Berrett-Koehler, 2002.

Zukav, Gary. *Soul Stories.* New York: Simon and Schuster, 2000.